# The Living Classroom

## Writing,
## Reading,
## and Beyond

**David Armington**

**with a foreword by Joseph Featherstone**

A 1996–97 NAEYC Comprehensive Membership Benefit

**National Association for the Education of Young Children**
**Washington, D.C.**

Regarding the samples of children's work in this book:

The names of children have been changed throughout this book, except where the name is an integral part of the child's artwork.

In doing their illustrated stories the children generally chose to use colored felt pens. Except for the cover art and the artwork between pages 106 and 107, the children's illustrations are reproduced in black and white. All are scaled down from their original size.

The drawings in Chapter 1 were done by the class of 1993, inspired by Jeanette's reading of Rosemary's "story" to them.

The artwork sprinkled throughout Chapter 4 was also done by the class of 1993. Having been told about this book in progress, the children decorated the margins of sample pages from the text. The designs were done in pencil. For most of the children this was a first-time art experience using that medium only.

The drawings at the end of Chapter 4 were done during the 1996–97 school year by the children in Donna LaRoche's first grade class.

**National Association for the Education of Young Children**
**1509 16th Street, NW**
**Washington, DC 20036-1426**
**202-232-8777 or 800-424-2460**
**Website http://www.naeyc.org/naeyc**

The National Association for the Education of Young Children (NAEYC) attempts through its publications program to provide a forum for discussion of major issues and ideas in our field. We hope to provoke thought and promote professional growth. The views expressed or implied are not necessarily those of the Association. NAEYC wishes to thank the author, who donated much time and effort to develop this book as a contribution to our profession.

Library of Congress Catalog Card Number: 97-69846
ISBN Number: 0-935989-83-8
NAEYC #174

*Design:* Kevin Jones; *Production:* Donna Weiss and Jack Zibulsky

**Printed in the United States of America.**

*for the grandchildren*

# CONTENTS

ACKNOWLEDGMENTS ............................................................... *vii*

FOREWORD ....................................................................... *ix*

INTRODUCTION ..................................................................... *1*

**1**   JEANETTE'S CLASSROOM ............................................... *7*
*– an action report by a frequent visitor –*

**2**   LEARNING TO "TALK" IN A NEW LANGUAGE ............... *17*
*– children's inventions as a stimulus to writing –*

**3**   A LOT ON THEIR MINDS ............................................... *47*
*– a closer look at the work of the children –*

**4**   THE LARGER PICTURE ................................................. *109*
*– we talk with Jeanette about children, learning, and teaching –*

"ALL KINDS OF CELEBRATIONS–AND SAD TIMES TOO" .............. *113*
*– about curriculum –*

"SERIOUS PURPOSE, NATURAL HONESTY, AND JOY" ................... *138*
*– about things social and emotional –*

"RECOGNIZING THE REACH OF THEIR MINDS" .......................... *156*
*– about learning "the skills" of reading and writing –*

**5**   REFLECTIONS ............................................................... *183*

EPILOGUE ...................................................................... *219*

BACKGROUND READINGS .................................................. *223*

# ACKNOWLEDGMENTS

This work of personal research, classroom-based, draws in substantial ways on a background of experience in teaching, curriculum development, and administration that goes back many years. Many individuals have contributed to my thinking about children, learning, and education, and to all of them I am most grateful:

Professional colleagues at the Hawken School in Cleveland, Ohio, during the years 1949–64;

Close friends and fellow researchers into children's thinking and learning, during the seminal days of curriculum development in the 1960s;

Certain teachers, advisers, and administrators in the County of Leicestershire, England, who welcomed me to their schools and classrooms on my several visits during the 1960s and who, over the years, facilitated cooperative endeavors on both sides of the ocean;

Colleagues on the staff of the Follow Through Project of the Education Development Center during the years 1968–70, and the many teachers, administrators, and parents of the EDC Follow Through communities who welcomed us to their schools and classrooms during those years;

A special group of children and their parents in Conway, New Hampshire, during school year 1972–73.

With respect to the development of the manuscript I wish to acknowledge the vital participation of Jeanette Amidon and my wife Rosemary, whose knowledge and experience in early childhood education and commitment to the project have made it, from the beginning, a truly cooperative endeavor. In addition, I wish to thank several individuals for reading the manuscript and responding with helpful suggestions: Carol Chomsky and Charles Temple for help in tightening the presentation of invented spelling; Monroe Cohen for suggestions about the presentation of the children's artwork; Bill and Sara Hull for their continuing interest, always constructive criticism, and encouragement; and the late John Holt for editorial tailoring combined with philosophical perspective. I also wish to thank Charna Levine and Vivian Zamel for their perspectives on Jeanette Amidon's classroom and developmental learning, and Melissa Elliot Griffith for her perspective on being a parent of a child in that classroom.

To our friends Jay and Helen Featherstone, parents extraordinaire, and their delightful family, I credit much inspiration and many fine lessons in storytelling and other good conversational practices that enrich the life of both family and friends.

In producing the book I am grateful to my designer, Kevin Jones, whose keen interest, sense of style, and command of computer power added greatly to my own learning and to my joy throughout the process; and to Carol Copple, my editor at NAEYC, whose knowledge of children and the educational process and delight in the manuscript gave special force to her suggestions for its improvement. I wish, finally, to acknowledge the late Robert Blaney, formerly principal of Winn Brook Elementary School, and Douglas Weinstock, the current principal, who always welcomed me to their school, and whose support of Jeanette Amidon has made it possible for her to have such report-worthy adventures in teaching.

# FOREWORD

Let's begin with a kid's drawing—the one on the book cover. The sun in person, wearing its lucky hair ribbon, is pouring a big syrupy rainbow down on boats, human figures and the creatures of the sea. The picture captures a moment of high life on our beautiful green and blue globe—a planetary party, really. It's gorgeous, the product of an artistic imagination with nerve to eat a world like an apple. Next, let's read a sentence in a book written by young Billy, whose father has died of cancer: "I wrote this book because I think a lot of people have a lot of pain—and that's the truth."

Do you have children? Do you wish other people's kids well? If so, I think you would like them to be part of a first grade classroom like Jeanette Amidon's in Belmont, Massachusetts. Room 101 is a place where first graders feel encouraged to speak and paint and write powerfully and for real purposes, to be skilled at creating certain tangible products—this wonderful rainbow picture, Billy's understated Book of Pain. A deeper skill is involved; these children are mastering the further conditions of growth. They are helping to create an intricate curriculum grounded in a profound reflectiveness about a world they have a hand in making. With luck this mastery—these habits of mind—will be theirs for the long run.

*The Living Classroom* is a book about how one teacher is able to enact—to make manifest—a value. The value could be called love or respect, except I'm afraid that to do so would be to lead readers into a familiar haze of anti-intellectual sentimentality. This anti-intellectual haze is one barrier to rethinking education. Let's be precise, intellectual. This book documents an approach to children's thinking; the root value in Room 101 is in fact respect for children's ideas. The children's works are the outward and visible signs of a teacher's respect for their thinking.

In the words of one observer, Ms. Amidon pays attention to what the kids are paying attention to. She does this so thoroughly and insistently and in such a well-organized classroom—a place arranged to capitalize on the luck of the day—that ordinary first graders find their intellectual power deepening in a hundred ways, including many that most schools and parents prize highly: the command of written expression, for example.

By paying passionate attention—by figuring out ways both to see and to help—Ms. Amidon makes enacting humane intellectual values the center of teaching. Her vivid example argues the case for what might be called a broad, cultural view of teaching. In this view, teaching children is not only or mainly the challenge of imparting specific skills, but rather a whole approach to living together as a small provisional classroom community dedicated to the development of ideas. Jeanette Amidon's version of teaching involves a joint commitment on the part of teacher and kids to "activity of thought and receptiveness to beauty and humane feeling" that Alfred North Whitehead years ago packed like a dynamite stick into a single word: culture.

This is a first grade classroom in which kids are learning to make, criticize, and renew humane intellectual culture. On this account alone it ought to be a very big story for a nation locked in uneasy cycles of confused and often trivial school reform. It confidently answers the biggest, usually unasked question about school reform: what's the point? *The Living Classroom* answers by showing, not just telling. It is an all too rare opportunity to listen to a gifted practitioner thinking out loud in the company of David and Rosemary Armington.

The Armingtons are themselves no slouches as teachers and observers. Rosemary Armington ran an outstanding primary school in Leicestershire, England, and has worked with teachers and kids in many different U.S. settings. David Armington is a veteran U.S. teacher with a long-standing interest in math. At one time, both worked in a creative variation of the federal Follow Through program, yet another good set of educational ideas that was tried with some acclaim and then abandoned by shifting fashions.

These two veterans speak to us about practice with the authority of success: they know from their own experience how teachers who are neither saints nor heroes can help all sorts of kids flourish in this style of active learning. The Armingtons also speak with what F. Scott Fitzgerald once called the authority of failure: they know what it is like to do superb work with children, to win the applause of parents, and yet to find themselves caught up in the school wars that are such a pronounced feature of the U.S. landscape. Their story—in the far background of this glowing portrait—reminds us of all the Jeanette Amidons who have left teaching or have been forced to leave over the past twenty years. Finding support to do good work that runs against the conventional grain is not easy. It may well be getting more difficult. The Armingtons remind us of what a wasteful country we are, educationally, careless of the treasuries of experience of good veteran teachers. I sometimes call it the United States of Amnesia.

The focus here is, however, Jeanette Amidon and the work she and the children do together. It's fascinating to see Ms. Amidon stepping on and off her high horse every few minutes, performing like some zany mixture of cook, janitor, and poet: she moves from the costumes for a class play to a hurt feeling to the fate of the human race, and then back to the felt-tip pen on which the universe balances.

I mention the pens again. They are no small matter. Felt-tip pens, Ms. Amidon argues in one revealing aside, make writing and drawing so much easier for first graders. They permit the stuff to flow—a key word—from fingertips and hands. They might be a good symbol for this whole operation. Kids don't learn from experience alone—that is a cliché, an educational bumper sticker. Raw experience often teaches nothing but confusion. Like the rest of us, kids really learn by reflecting on experience. Helping them reflect should be the basic job of teaching.

The way to do this best is by some teetering mix: a chance to do, to mess around, to experiment, and then reflect, either in talk or on paper or some other medium. Then back again for more experience to interrogate. Not one thing, but more than one thing, constantly reblended: the collision of raw material and reflection in the form of talk and writing and representation. It's important to keep this flow flowing—a teacher is performing when this happens, and managing the flow well from hour to hour may be the real heart of Jeanette Amidon's skill. The result of living in such a flow is a habit of mind, the confident capacity to interrogate experience constantly. Its possession is worth more than pearls and rubies. For first graders, as well as sophomores in college, the critical flow—the flow that swims to the top of all the other flowing things—is the flow of ideas.

Pens are means and metaphor for the ongoing river of reflection that makes Room 101 a fine place for children's minds. The pens are accessible to little kids, like phonetic spelling itself, which also allows their existing power over language to flow readily into ideas and reflection and a new skill: writing. Hard intellectual work, under such conditions, comes easy. You might even say it flows. This handsomely illustrated book must surely be the finest tribute to the felt-tip pen industry in the entire English language.

The natural first thing for any reader of this text will be to look at what the kids have produced with these pens: the witty drawings, the stories with increasingly sophisticated invented spelling in Chapter 2, the intelligent designs, the musical interlude, math work, the sketches for plays, and all the rest. This is in fact a good place to start, a feast for eyes and mind. It would be a great mistake to linger on the products, however. Like most cultural artifacts, these need interpreting. They arise out of a world of interrogated experience that Ms. Amidon and the children shape together. The children's work this book displays so beautifully are only the tip of a vast iceberg.

One part of the iceberg you can't see is a developmental philosophy about children and the best conditions for their growth. The real hero in this classroom is not the Book of Pain, or even Billy or Celeste, but the power of growth itself, which, with thoughtful guidance, takes the kids along on its strong current past even the death of a father on into the life of the imagination. Throughout this book there is a focus on an approach to children that constantly builds a bridge from existing strengths to new learning. Ms. Amidon has faith in kids' power to generate serious ideas and worthy art. She conveys to kids that with her help they will take the next step and then the next after that.

And they do, even when the range is narrow and the stories are obsessional. The writing and art show the deep truth that Sigmund Freud stumbled on before he went on to more debatable conclusions: we are each of us the poet and artist of our own stories. Teaching that doesn't capitalize on this basic human fact is less powerful than teaching that taps into people's stories—in first grade, or in graduate seminars.

After paging through this testimony, think a little about the kind of classroom life these stories represent, and then take them to the next public educational meeting in your community. Show them around with little commentary. When was the last time you heard our national educational walruses speak about children's strengths as the core of the enterprise of learning? When did you ever hear a superintendent in one of our school systems say that faith in the children is the foundation of the curriculum? I pose my questions rhetorically—I know the answer. Too many of our schools run on organized mistrust. There are severe shortages of felt-tip pens, good talk, rich experience, and real books—scope, in a word, for the imagination.

"Teaching children to think," like "teaching for understanding," is one of the earnest goals of today's earnest school reformers, especially those based in the universities. Jeanette Amidon is here to remind them that children are already thinking, thank you very much. It's the job of teachers to tap into this great and renewable—potentially infinite—resource.

How she does this is, of course, the question, to which there can be no single answer. This in itself is an important point: there is no one best system. The pursuit of the one best system is part of the traditional pathology of U.S. schools. What counts is not any one activity or thing but rather a developmental philosophy, an approach to working with kids, daily routines that respect mind and feelings through the exercise of what Frances Hawkins calls the logic of action.

No ideas but in things, William Carlos Williams once said about poetry—meaning that the concrete things energize a poem, whereas abstractions weaken its magnetic field. This holds for classroom teaching too. Take the abstraction *respect,* for example, so central to the creation of a good intellectual community. A lot of adults really do respect children, but they are baffled at how to make respect manifest on a daily basis and even more baffled at how to enact a respect for children's minds as a routine matter.

Intangible respect hovers in the air of our schoolrooms like an unfulfilled romance or an unsent letter. Meanwhile too many of our schools continue as profoundly disrespectful environments for everybody involved—grown-ups as well as kids. We could all take lessons from Ms. Amidon. When the guppy dies, the response is swift: "We need a meeting." There is discussion, reflection, and then action. Language has direct purposes and concrete uses. No respect, Dr. Williams might say, but in visible acts of respect.

Pedagogically, Ms. Amidon's work represents a variation on a classic tradition that is sometimes called progressive education. I myself am still looking for the right label. "Progressive education" sounds dated, and besides, it always has a whiff of the unintended comedy captured by the famous New Yorker cartoon: "Teacher, do we have to do what we want to do again today?"

In the '60s and '70s, when "open education" was much to the fore—generating a body of remarkable creative work that is still part of the working pedagogical capital in many schools—I tried to get people to march under a banner I labeled "decent schools." I had no luck at all. Maybe the truth is that if you deal in labels too much you end up in the gumming business. Whatever the labels, certain classic ideas are present here, made alive all over again as though rinsed by the fresh start that is young children's ongoing gift to a tired world.

One is the idea that a child learns well from experiences in which she has a vital stake, some genuine interest. Another is that much quality learning—learning that you can build on, that sticks to your bones—involves authentic performance: doing something real. Writing, for example, should be a means of saying something you want or need to say to some audience. It works less well as a school exercise you are doing because a large credentialed person orders you to do so. A third is the idea that a certain amount of the curriculum—a very great deal in Jeanette Amidon's case—can arise from a continuous reconstruction of experience generated by the ongoing activities of children. This doesn't just happen; it results from careful teaching: the teacher has to be organizer, catalyst, curriculum developer, and conductor.

A fourth idea is the importance of capitalizing on individual differences—not just accepting the intractable billiness of Billy, but taking advantage of it in a way that advances Billy's mind and his powers by tapping into his interests and his big stories—helping Billy make an education in which he can see his stories nested in wider stories about the world. A fifth idea is the collective power of common learning: the capacity of groups of children, under a teacher's guidance, to turn their shared conversation and insight and activities into a social medium of learning, so that a classroom becomes more than the sum of its individual parts, and children teach each other in an ongoing dialogue, creating a common classroom culture of ideas.

Every one of these ambitious ideas is in effect a large criticism of conventional schooling. Every single one has been enacted in some time and place by ordinary teachers—with the right support—in classrooms with all kinds of kids. People like me and Jeanette Amidon and the authors of this book have been pushing them for some years, and we are relative newcomers. Teaching this way is definitely not something new. It's actually one version of traditional education—going back at least as far as the founding of public education. Educational talk usually pits each new round of the New Education (this generation's version of progressive practice) against something called traditional education. It would be more accurate to say that the varieties of progressive practice from the 1820s on are a cumulative, dissenting tradition that stands in contrast to the lockstep and factory style that has won out in much public schooling.

This is traditional education too. In each generation since roughly the 1820s, thoughtful teachers in both public and private settings in many countries have discovered ways of working with children that are better than batch processing and organized boredom. Often their work has been part of a dialogue with parents who were slowly democratizing child-rearing and making family life more of a conversation. This tradition of conversational practice and children's active learning—what we might call the democracy of experience—has not failed, though many obituaries have been printed. Although difficult to do, and making great demands on teachers, this style of teaching has often succeeded, and in fact has influenced schools a good deal—especially practice with younger children. And of course it has had an effect on families over the last few generations.

By now this counter tradition of respect for kids' minds has accumulated an impressive record with all sorts of children on many continents. The tradition tends to be most at home with young children and the early years of school—Jeanette Amidon's work is classic. And it is true that the most widespread practice in the '60s and '70s was in the elementary schools. (Although there is a history of superb high school and college work that is slowly getting forgotten, too.) One unfortunate by-product of recent reform movements from the point of view of those of us interested in kids' creativity is that reformers have pressured the elementary schools to become more boring. Environments that were once good for little children become as deadly and sterile as the high school up the street.

This may be the reason why I am tempted now to write the word "reform" in quotation marks. If school reform means no more recess for children, then I am no reformer. The reign of quantitative testing continues, even as the scientific foundation propping up the tests has eroded. Thoughtful people are exploring alternative means of assessment. Some "policy" groups are almost beginning to catch up to the lifetime wisdom of the legendary Miss Jones, an enormously influential teacher in Rosemary Armington's superb Westfield School in Leicestershire, England. "Children," she once assured a group of American visitors, "do not get any heavier for being weighed."

Jeanette Amidon, like the Armingtons, is in part a product of open education and its earlier British cousins. Much U.S. reform of the '60s and '70s—inspired by teachers and parents, or projects like the federal Follow Through program, or the early years of Head Start—reflected vital and creative work in U.S. education. Their example could offer important clues for genuine school reform today. Ms. Amidon might be said to speak for several generations of school veterans who have struggled to advance a vision of children's imaginations on into times when children count for less and less in the nation's concerns.

Of course there are always problems in moving an approach that began with young learners up into classrooms with older kids. Open education often floundered when it came to making the intellectual connections necessary for the curriculum in the later years of school. Still, there has been enough success with the later years of schooling to build on. In some lucky places, teachers have succeeded. The real problems remain matters of value—fundamental views of how children best learn. David Armington speaks of some of the difficulties of promoting active learning with older kids. He points to a pretty common attitude: it may be okay for little kids to learn through play, but the idea that all students require serious play—that such play is the essence of intellectual life—is a hard sell in an anti-intellectual nation where the Puritan hangover keeps hanging over. The fear of big kids and their energy in this culture is one of its least attractive features.

Still, many of us see small, hopeful signs. There is a lot of ferment in schools these days, and a great deal of fresh interest in children's thinking. Kids' writing has been undergoing a renaissance for some time now. Jeanette Amidon's approach is not as rare as it once was. Real books are making inroads, where pinched school budgets allow. The idea that math should be a conversation about ideas has gotten a huge impetus from new math standards, which in turn reflect some very creative classroom practice. A host of today's efforts reflect another new round of a good old idea: that children can construct intelligent meanings.

Evaluation is getting another look. Some are starting to see the sense in Pat Carini's long-standing contention that the root of the word "evaluation" is "value." The question of what values we wish to enact is central to assessment. If you want to test splinter skills instead of real reading and real writing, then you are placing a value on splinters and slices instead of the whole, live hog. Parents and activists in poor communities are mutinying, as they should, and many are looking for alternatives. Many middle-class parents constitute a potential clientele for progressive practice. Some systems are scurrying to provide options for students within a responsible public framework, as many of the charter schools do. You hear the sound of some new fiddles playing old tunes. The long worldwide quest for alternatives to lockstep teaching may be resuming its hesitant U.S. march.

I agree with David Armington that rigid U.S. school systems need an American version of *perestroika,* although I am deeply worried about recent calls for privatizing education and turning public schools over to the mercies of the free market. In the free market the rich get richer and the poor poorer. With education, as with health care, we need a common system. Whether we will get one in a nation more and more divided by what Jonathan Kozol calls "savage inequalities" is, alas, an open question. Armington is right to point to experiments with parental choice within public systems as a promising development.

I connect many promising stirrings in education today to a wider uprising against Mr. Gradgrind, the utilitarian capitalist who has hogged the microphone in this country for far longer than his turn. Charles Dickens created him in the 19th century, but he is now alive and well in America, where his investments in human greed have prospered mightily. Mr. Gradgrind is the arch bean counter of all time. He believes in teaching only facts, facts, facts. He is suspicious of appeals to children's imaginations. He does not want children to have ideas, or think for themselves, or have fun. He would call Jeanette Amidon's class a circus and an anarchy. He and his loyal ally, the Rev. Gradgrind, are out to destroy public education, partly because they are ideologues promoting private enterprise and unchecked competition, but mostly because they fear strong free minds.

Mr. Gradgrind does well by calculating alone; children mostly do not. That is why, in each generation, Gradgrind's one best system of education done on the cheap is actually a huge, costly failure. The developmental ideas captured so well in Jeanette Amidon's work— whatever their considerable difficulties—have the merit of conforming to children's nature. They are complex and subtle ideas, but they are more practical and realistic in the long run than Mr. Gradgrind's sentimental illusions of control.

If there is one thread linking some of the hopeful educational developments in our often bleak landscape, it's the belief that an education suited to children's nature is in fact possible and that classrooms can provide opportunities for—above all—intelligent reflection on experiences that matter. Children's thinking—the serious play of all truly intellectual work—is the watchword of much of the best current practice, as well as the academic theory that is limping as it tries to catch up to practitioners like Jeanette Amidon. It's time to revise the reigning clichés again. A nation, after all, is judged by its clichés. They are in effect our working conjectures about daily life and our institutions. We would be much better off if we exchanged Gradgrind's clichés for the promising conjecture that teachers will succeed better of they pay attention to children's ideas.

It's significant that interesting progressive practice is emerging in the public schools, and even more significant to see it appearing in a handful of public high schools and junior highs. At Central Park East high school, for instance, you will see some remarkable parallels with Jeanette Amidon's practice.

This is no coincidence. Deborah Meier, the famous founder of Central Park East, an alternative public high school in New York City, has set a new and demanding intellectual standard for high schools. Like Jeanette Amidon, she is a product of progressive preschool movements, "open education," and its successors. She often says, smiling, that what she wants for kids in New York City is a mix of the only two educational institutions in which real ideas and your own interests really mesh: kindergarten and the elite graduate schools. In between, she argues, students do not generally pursue their own interests or learn how to take ideas seriously. Much in-between education tries to ignore who you are and the fact that you have a mind of your own. (As a university professor, I think she may be romanticizing the graduate schools, but I take her point.)

Of course the point strikes home because most of Central Park East's students are poor ("inner city"). The children of the poor are not often supposed to have ideas. It jars expectations to see poor students, many of color, who have views about whether or not Columbus was a true Renaissance Man or whether *King Lear* is a better play than *Macbeth*. Like Vivian Paley, Deborah Meier offers us big news: fresh images of a teaching practice that takes children's minds seriously, enacting respect for ideas as a routine classroom matter. This is the bread our children are hungry for. Growing numbers of classroom teachers are making their voices heard on these same themes—in itself a refreshing departure from educational discussions dominated by those who spend little time in real classrooms. Now, thanks to David Armington, we can add Jeanette Amidon to the growing list of practical classroom visionaries.

It should go without saying, but I must add, that this book will fail completely in its intent if it is taken as a text on invented spelling. Think of spelling as a metaphor, like the felt-tip pens. It's a metaphor for a way of working from kids' masteries—what they already know—toward new learning. That's the generic secret, the two-way traffic between kids' experience and the school curriculum, and then back again, the bridge with all the ongoing reflections in its moving waters. We are speaking, as I have spoken, of a developmental approach, a philosophy, values in action across the entire curriculum.

If children can tap into their native powers of language while exploring the mysteries of English spelling—if they can end up with a better command of language, why isn't similar exploration possible in all the other parts of the curriculum? What happens here with spelling could happen in math, for example: why do you borrow when the number you are subtracting is too big? Is this the sort of thing children can explore profitably, with the rest of the class, or is it a sacred topic, reserved only for the powerful keepers of the society's mysteries and algorithms? Is there a value in spending time so children come to identify themselves as the sort of people who solve problems and figure things out through the habit of mind of purposeful, intelligent talk? What sort of people do we want our kids to become? What sort of society should they make? *The Living Classroom* points us to the real basics in education.

Lastly, a simple point that gets lost in the rivers of anxious words. Hundreds of thousands of children are bored stiff in our schools. This would be a crisis if it weren't somehow normal. Jeanette Amidon's children love what they are doing. How, as someone says in these pages, did learning to read ever get to be such a grim business? Pin up this sentence on the wall of your school board: "Enjoyment seems to be the key."

– *Joseph Featherstone*
Michigan State University
April 1997

# INTRODUCTION

Aside from the children whose work is featured here, the leading character of our narrative is their classroom teacher, Jeanette Amidon. For those readers who are interested in helping children learn to write and may already know about "invented spelling," Jeanette's classroom may suggest ways in which such early experiences in literacy can be enriched and extended. For those readers who are interested in the teaching of reading and are familiar with the perennial argument over phonics versus whole language methods, Jeanette's classroom experience may suggest a naturalistic resolution to this controversy, a blending of the useful features of both approaches in ways that help children remain in charge of their own learning. For those readers who are comfortable, as perhaps most parents are, with the idea that young children learn best through informal activities and play during the preschool years, Jeanette's classroom offers a glimpse of how the vitality and power of children's early learning can be sustained in the more formal settings of school, and how a curriculum emerging from children's ideas can be organic to the development of vital skills and values. For those readers accustomed to thinking that children with "special needs" require special treatment in segregated classes, Jeanette's heterogeneous mix of children may suggest that all children's needs are special and that a good informal classroom provides a workable way to accommodate them. For that growing number of educational reformers who are attracted to the idea of parental choice as a way of fixing America's schools, it must be emphasized that this book highlights educational ideas and practices that represent a truly significant alternative to those that prevail in most schools today. Finally, for those presently involved in creative forms of innovation and experimentation in today's schools, I would hope that our discussion of life in this particular first grade, and its wider implications, might serve as a contribution to the healthy intellectual ferment about education now evident in many parts of the nation.

One further comment may be useful by way of orientation to the reader. Since 1976 when Jeanette Amidon first began teaching in Room 101 at the Winn Brook School in Belmont, Massachusetts, her classroom has seen a steady stream of visitors: parents, teachers, school administrators, researchers and writers, filmmakers, in addition to the flow of apprentice teachers from local training colleges selected by their professors each year to work in her classroom. It is almost impossible not to enjoy a stay in this room, even if you're used to, and believe in, a much more tightly structured teaching situation, but experience shows that what these visitors take with them by way of impressions can vary widely. Some, who respond enthusiastically to Jeanette's way of working with children, see her as some kind of model and go away inspired to try and imitate her. Others, probably more, see her as one of those rare and admirable talents from whom we can learn little because they are simply too special. Still others see her as an extraordinarily skilled practitioner in doing informally what most other first grade teachers prefer to do more formally—namely, teach children to read, write, and do simple math.

I regard all of these views, while understandable, as essentially wide of the mark, for to fully appreciate Jeanette's classroom is to comprehend its underpinnings in the principles of child development, principles rooted in more than a century of sound early childhood education practice, and in recent decades ever more widely validated by scientific research. Jeanette Amidon is neither a model, nor a miracle, nor simply a method smith. What she does, other "developmentally minded" adults can do, and are doing, but in their own highly personal ways. As one of Jeanette's teacher training professors remarked to me recently: "Development is development;

if you understand how it works in us—and I don't mean just in children—you'll respect certain principles and avoid doing certain things that are really pretty foolish." We hope that some of these principles will shine forth through the pages of this book and that at least some of the foolish things we do to children (and perhaps even to ourselves) in the name of education may become more apparent.

In various ways this book dips into the ongoing personal research of three people: Jeanette Amidon, my wife Rosemary, and myself. All of us have spent many years in classrooms with young children. We come together here to investigate some of the work of Jeanette's children, to reflect on it and on the conditions under which it was produced. Our aim is to learn more about how children learn, by letting the children themselves teach us. The book represents the visible part of an ongoing dialogue that began many years ago. We hope readers will involve themselves in the book as though they were being invited to participate in the dialogue. Perhaps they will think about some of the children they know as we talk about children we know.

Rosemary and I first met Jeanette Amidon in 1969 when we were members of a small team of teachers working on a research project of the U.S. Office of Education. The purpose of the project, known as Follow Through, was to provide ongoing support to "graduates" of Head Start programs as these children entered kindergarten and the primary grades. The government plan was to achieve this support by garnering a group of "experts" representing different approaches to early childhood education, to invite participating school districts (all in poverty areas) to sign on with the expert whose approach most appealed to the administrators, teachers, and parents of that district, who would then agree to accept that expert's consultant services for a period of years (i.e., until the government money ran out!), during which time, and after which, the relative impacts of these various approaches would be assessed by reputable independent evaluators.

As for the research results of the Follow Through Project, which lasted, officially, until 1978, these were, to my knowledge, inconclusive. None of the so-called "models" proved itself clearly superior to any other in helping children learn "the skills," which is primarily what the testers were testing. Less measurable objectives, such as creativity, problem-solving, and the capacity for self-direction—high on our list of priorities—did not figure in the statistical evaluations.

After three years with the research project Jeanette, Rosemary, and I went back to the classroom. We felt that we had been itinerant "experts" long enough, visiting all those schools and trying to support people struggling to make schools better. We wanted to get back to the classroom, to get close to children again and to continue our own learning. Jeanette took several different teaching jobs, variously disappointing, before hearing of the opening in Belmont in 1976. There, at the Winn Brook School, she met principal Robert Blaney, whose educational values reflecting his deep sensitivity to children convinced her that she would have the support and cover she needed to teach according to her convictions. And so in this fairly traditional school, in a conservative middle-class community, at a time when the public wanted the "basics," Jeanette Amidon began to run a nontraditional classroom, with Mr. Blaney's quiet but firm support. The other vital support came from the parents of children in Jeanette's classes. They liked what they saw happening to their children, and they liked being part of the action—Jeanette has always encouraged parents to spend time in her classroom. When Mr. Blaney retired, Douglas Weinstock took his place and continued the support that enables Jeanette to keep right on doing what she enjoys and believes in.

From the beginning Rosemary and I were interested in Jeanette's classroom, because we knew we would be welcome there and would enjoy interacting with the children and being part of the informality of the group for as long as we cared to stay. I personally had a more specific interest as well. I saw her room as a place where I could introduce informally some of the math materials I had designed, to see what appeal they might have. After several visits I saw that this work was going fairly well, but quite suddenly other even more exciting things began to happen—in the area of language, specifically with the children's writing.

Jeanette had recently met Carol Chomsky, the linguist, and had read several of Carol's articles describing how young children, often before they read, will frequently try to scribble something in writing and in the process "invent" ways to spell the words they want to use. At about that same time Debra Cheney, one of Rosemary's graduate students (Rosemary was then teaching at the University of New Hampshire) had also read Carol's work and was noting how some of the children in her preschool group were making up stories and were inventing ways to spell the words. Jeanette visited Debra's class, was intrigued by what she saw happening, and decided to "have a go" with her own first graders. The results were almost immediately transforming of the children's desire to express themselves on paper—they could hardly wait to get to school to "write" their stories. From her experience Jeanette sensed that something developmentally important was going on, with practical implications for children's growth into literacy.

For me the children's explosion into writing, with the organic linkages to reading that developed during that year, came as a possible breakthrough on a problem that had bothered me for many years: why does learning to read have to be such grim work for so many children and their teachers? For five years they've been learning incredibly complex things without adults managing every step of the process. So, why, in the first grade, do we suddenly have to sit children down and teach them reading and writing with such a heavy hand? A respected colleague and notably competent first grade teacher, whose experience was in the formal tradition, once chided me by saying: "You can give your sixth graders all that freedom and do all those exciting things with them because we've taught them to *read* here in the first grade. They've got to get the skills first, and that's our job." I now see Jeanette's kind of classroom as a compelling response to that colleague, because in such a classroom freedom and excitement in learning do indeed combine with a serious and workable orientation toward the acquisition of literacy.

It is perhaps not surprising that many of our best teachers and most insightful observers of children are not writers or do not choose to write, but there may be other ways for them to speak. I'm sure there will always be things we can learn from them, if we can find ways of tuning in to what they know, intuitively if not consciously, at the deeper levels of their craft. We need to tap that wisdom, about children and about learning—things idiosyncratic and personal to one teacher's art, as well as things that have general truth and wide application, things useful to learners everywhere. Over the years Jeanette Amidon has resisted writing about her work; she much prefers to talk about it. This book gives her that opportunity. As faithfully as we can tell it, this book is Jeanette's story.

# 1

# JEANETTE'S CLASSROOM

*– an action report by a frequent visitor –*

Over the years my wife Rosemary has visited Jeanette Amidon's room many times. On this one occasion she wrote a description, as part of a series of observational papers that she was doing in connection with her teaching at the University of New Hampshire. For me her description goes a long way toward capturing the spirit of the class and the way Jeanette works with the children. The reader should be warned that Rosemary does nothing to conceal her enthusiasm and biases as an observer.

**Rosemary.** Since David has made clear that my observations are biased as well as enthusiastic, I should perhaps explain where my biases come from: I grew up with them! The teacher training that I received at college in England many years ago had rooted me firmly in what are called "developmental principles" of learning. When I first found myself with my own class of young children, three- and four-years old, many of the experienced teachers that surrounded me were putting these principles into practice. Words like "child-centered," "discovery," "interest," "curiosity," "choice," "self-direction," "play"—my college vocabulary—took on fresh meaning as I worked with the children for whom I was responsible. Later I became headmistress of an "infant school" (children aged five to seven) in Leicestershire, a county where the prevailing climate was one of trust and support. Here I learned much more about what it is like to have my professional contribution respected and to have our school encouraged to grow in its own highly personal and individual way. In short, I felt that I belonged to a profession that was expected to make a unique contribution to the accumulating knowledge about how children learn and the conditions under which they learn best. It was that expectation that dignified our practice, strengthened our resolve, and immeasurably improved our schools.

I feel at home and comfortable in Jeanette's classroom and in others like it. I find it easy to become part of the life there, challenging to try to help the children forward in their learning, exciting to take home with me fresh incidents to discuss, new insights to share, and more evidence about the way adults as well as children learn. It is not easy to cut through the busy life of such a classroom, to present incidents that capture its intensity and flow and that do justice to its underlying values. What a child may be doing at any time is related to what he or she has just done and will soon be doing. I find these connections missing from my account, as I miss many of them myself in a brief visit. But perhaps something of the spirit of the classroom will come through—and the serious yet joyful purposes of the children.

Jeanette's first grade classroom is off the long straight hallway of an elementary school. Outside her open door I notice several children decorating the bulletin board. A display of various creative efforts is in the process of being mounted by three six-year-olds.

"What about this?" says one.

"That's Andy's. I think it's a cement mixer; he's making a label for it."

They tape Andy's mixer to the board.

"That's a very interesting display," I say.

"It's called Inventions," says Melanie, "this week's inventions."

I notice the strange collection on the table in the hallway. Not without reason does Jeanette refer to herself from time to time as "the junk lady." I examine Andy's "cement truck" made from toilet roll cores, plastic caps, assorted boxes, and tape. Fisher-Price toys were never like this! I pause in the doorway of Jeanette's classroom, as I often do.

"Hi, Mrs, Armington, see what I made." Rosanna is Chinese, and she is wearing a mortarboard and trailing a kite. Not a real mortarboard or a real kite. More inventions. And very well done.

"I like your hat, Rosanna."

"It's not a hat—it's a mortarboard," she replies with some dignity.

"Is a mortarboard a hat?" I ask.

She considers my question seriously, then with a slow smile she says, "I guess it's both. Help me find somewhere to dry my kite."

We find the ideal place, a clothesline strung across the classroom, a windlass at each end. At six-inch intervals there are loops, and from many of these are suspended removable formica squares with numerals. I notice a pattern—3, 6, 9, 12, 15, 18. Jonathan sees my interest.

"I'm learning to count in different ways," he says. "I'm working on 3s. I've done my 5s but we ran out of loops, so I had to pretend loops in my head. I got to 275."

I think of the usual first grade math curriculum: numbers from 1 to 10, or maybe 20. Big numbers are not usually the business of first grade. I think of dinosaurs and monsters. Bigness can be fascinating when you're only six.

"How do you do it, Jonathan?" I ask.

"Do what?"

"Work on big numbers like 275."

"We've got a lot of new stuff," he says, leading me over to a large low table.

"Can you show me 275?" I ask. He quickly picks up two large square wooden tiles, each painted a bright orange and marked off into a 10" X 10" grid.

"Here's 200," he says. Then he counts out seven 10-inch strips marked off into 1-inch squares.

"There's 70, and here's 5," he says, picking up five 1-inch squares. "I'm nearly as good as Hiroko at math, but she's best."

Hiroko hears her name and comes over. She's from Japan, small, with shiny straight black hair and spectacles perched on a tiny nose.

"David's showing me bases. We use base 10 because we have 10 fingers. I told David we would have to use base 20 if we counted our toes too."

She has an artless way of displaying her intelligence—no show off, just know-how.

"Math is easy for me," she says, "but writing is harder [she sighs] but I learn."

"Hiroko," a voice calls, and she's gone.

I turn around and almost fall over a large roll of paper about 12 inches wide that has been stretched across the floor from one end of the classroom to the middle. The roll at my feet is mounted on a homemade windlass, and Andy is laboring over the final details of its design and operation. Not the moment to interrupt, I think, and glance to the other end. Billy is holding that end of the roll. He grins at me.

"What are you making, Billy?"

"I don't know," he says, with refreshing frankness, "but I love to help Andy. He's such a great inventor—his things really work!"

Ah, Andy, I think, Andy of the cement mixer, obviously a privilege to work for such a fellow, even if you only hold the roll!

"How do you spell *sox*?" I hear. "Y'know, Red Sox."

Jeanette says, "How do you think it begins, Evan?"

"*S*."

"Yes, and what do you hear next?"

"*S* again."

"Write it then."

I glance over at Evan who is busy labeling his baseball picture. A group of children are writing books. Their talking, writing, and drawing flow from their mouths and fingers as they work. I sit down and Joanie comes over, book in hand. It has construction paper covers and several stapled sheets inside. She begins to read to me:

"The Book a Bot Rooddof the Red Noas Radr

"Mommy I don't wont this noas

"Fathr Rooddof dusit like his noas

"I doo no wut too doo."

I know that Joanie's illustrated story of Rudolph and the nose he doesn't like will probably be "published" by the Room 101 "press" and every child will get a copy. I think about each child's accumulating library. They each must have about 50 books by now. I look around the room and notice again all the evidence of correct spelling that surrounds the children and supports their efforts. The Tallest Tower in the World, a notice announces. Remember, We Have Only Four Earphones, So Four Children Only, Please, another says. Dinosaur Words Here, says the lid of a box.

I look again at the tallest tower and notice that it's part of a city of blocks. Many first grade teachers think that blocks are for kindergarten, but not Jeanette. I listen while Jamie tells me about their fantastic block city. Jamie has a severe speech handicap, and I need to pay sharp attention to catch his words.

"I've written a book about it," he says. He opens it and begins to read.

"Batman in my city. He's jumping down, down." He reads with much effort and much pride. When children really want to learn, they will go to such trouble to do things right. This is especially hard for Jamie, but he struggles on.

The soft tones of the piano interrupt my thoughts, and the children are gathering together around Jeanette.

"Today," she says, "Andy has brought something to share with us." Andy, the inventor, carefully unpacks a menorah. Jeanette encourages him to tell about it, and he does.

"Remember our Jewish song?" Jeanette asks. "Let's sing it, and Andy will show us how he will light the candles on his menorah."

Lucky Andy, I think—home experiences validated at school and, from all I hear, school experiences validated at home. The cement truck will go home to be treasured.

It's lunchtime, and Jeanette and I settle down to share our morning's observations and reflections. Suddenly a voice, shrill and urgent, intrudes:

"It's dead, it's dead, Mrs. Amidon—the big guppy, the very biggest, it's dead!"

Children filter back, excitement spreads. No doubt about it, the favorite guppy is dead.

"We need to bury him."

"We need a box to put him in."

"We need to sing a hymn."

"We need a funeral."

"We need a meeting!" Jeanette says firmly, and very soon order emerges from the chaos, and a group of children elect to take care of the burial rites. I notice that Jeanette elects to be around them, ready as a resource. No lesson planning here. I think of a book I know called *The Geranium on the Window Sill Just Died But Teacher You Went Right On.*[1] Teacher, the guppy in our tank just died and you stopped to listen. The undertakers line a minicoffin, dig a grave under the juniper bush, and put up a collection of intriguing signs.

The other children drift over to various projects, no doubt thankful that the burial rites are in such good hands. Soon the familiar sounds of relaxed but purposeful activity fill the air. Patrick is helping Andy paint his menorah onto the Christmas frieze—"cuz he's the only Jewish boy and he needs my help." I read a story to Martha and Joanne. We are sharing a cozy corner with Jennifer, who is deeply engrossed in her own book, and with Amy, who is slowly, word by word, reading aloud to herself. Jennifer learned to read early and easily, and Amy is only now beginning to make sense of those mysterious black squiggles.

---

[1] Albert Cullum, Harlin Quist, 1971.

The afternoon speeds past, and soon it's time to go home. Alicia dons her coat of many colors, walks to the blackboard, picks up a white chalk and writes, BYE MRS. AMIDON, I LOVE YOU, and she's gone. Her first school experience expressed in six small words. Jeanette checks her classroom mailbox.

Dear Mrs. Amidon

You r the bst teechr

in the wrld and I hop you nevr dy

Yor frend Beth

Jeanette sinks into the nearest chair. "I probably will, if I keep this up," she says with a grin.

Later that evening I'm reading through some of the books that the children have written, and at the same time I'm trying to find words to explain the underlying elements of this classroom that make it operate the way it does, that explain the combination of relaxation *and* involvement, of informality *and* respect, of freedom *and* stability. In a very real sense the children are in charge of their own learning, and much of the time they are charting their own course. Perhaps the stability and structure are there because the children willingly invest Jeanette with leadership and authority, because they know she knows more than they do, but equally important, they do this because all the signals they have ever received from her convey to them her respect for their growing powers and her trust that they will reach out and learn. These signals also convey to the children Jeanette's understanding, support, and even indulgence of their childhood. They feel safe to investigate, to experiment, to take risks, to accept challenges. They also feel safe to play, to fantasize, to laugh, to cry—to be children.

Dear Mrs. Amidon

I hope you never die!

Your friend,

Rosemary

\*      \*      \*

Rosemary's account of this one-day visit, revealing as it does a classroom of kaleidoscopic activity, may bring the reader to wonder about children's sustained attention in particular areas of curriculum and their work in these areas. An interested observer wishing to pick out for investigation one facet of Jeanette Amidon's classroom would have tantalizing options: the artwork or the music, the drama, or perhaps the math, the writing, or the reading. Perhaps some would be interested in the integration of non-English-speaking children, the use of adult volunteers, or the involvement of parents.

As I said in the Introduction, I have chosen to focus on Jeanette's approach to reading and writing because of my longtime interest in the development of literacy and because learning to read is so strongly emphasized in most first grades. In Chapter 2, I will examine in some detail children's "invented spelling" and the part it plays in the expression of their feelings and ideas through writing and drawing as they move toward literacy. In a subsequent chapter we will investigate this writing and discover that it is hitched to many other interesting and important things.

(Many readers may now be familiar with invented spelling as developmental behavior, and they may wish to skim Chapter 2. Those for whom the topic is new may appreciate the challenge of paying closer attention to the details.)

# 2

# *Learning to "Talk" in a New Language*

*– children's inventions as a stimulus to writing –*

From her earliest days as a teacher of young children Jeanette Amidon's approach has stemmed from well-established principles of child growth and development, principles embedded in much of what Rosemary observed during her visits. For many years, such principles have formed the underpinnings of good programs for children three, four, or even five years of age. They are indeed the principles behind a healthy home and community life for children. At the core of these principles is the idea that the human animal learns because it's built for learning: that the urge to learn and the capacity to learn come as standard equipment on all models, and that the equipment functions best in a stimulating and caring human environment. Jeanette believes, as do most early childhood specialists, that the powers children bring with them to school are already well developed, as evidenced by the learning that normally occurs during the first five years of life. Consider the intellectual feat of learning one's native language. (Chinese infants even learn to speak Chinese—incredible!)

**A Natural Way to Learn.** The challenge to primary school teachers (and indeed to all teachers) is not somehow to impart intellectual powers to children but to help them develop the powers they already have. In her teaching Jeanette has always taken seriously the idea that children's emerging abilities, those so evident in the years before school, can and should be brought to bear on all kinds of learning, including the learning of basic literacy skills. For many years she had used children's writing as a way of helping them into reading, because this seemed a natural way for them to learn. Several details of this approach are important as background for appreciating the important change that began to take place in 1976.

In her previous teaching Jeanette had encouraged her children to draw and write from their own experience, using whatever words each experience called for. No "controlled vocabulary" was used that would restrict expression. If a child wanted to write a word he didn't know how to spell (which happened often), he would try to find the correct spelling—perhaps by consulting one of the many word charts available in the room or by asking Jeanette or other available adult, or by looking in his own personal "dictionary," a stapled-together little booklet in which a growing list of "favorite words" could be kept, correctly spelled. Gradually many children built up a vocabulary of words they knew how to spell, thus becoming less dependent on these outside resources. Through this process they were also helped to acquire that "phonetic sense" which is so basic to competence in reading. Still, Jeanette thought that the children's need for correct spelling had restricting effects: their drawing tended to be restricted by what they knew they could write, their writing restricted by what they knew they could spell.

**A New Idea.**   In the introduction I mentioned that in 1976 Jeanette discovered a different way of thinking about this spelling "problem." She had recently read several of Carol Chomsky's articles on "invented spelling,"[1] and when Rosemary told her about Debra Cheney's preschool group in New Hampshire, she decided to visit Debra's class,[2] where a small group of children had recently become interested in "writing." Jeanette noticed that the children were paying close attention to some of the sounds in words they wanted to write and had "invented" quite sensible spellings:

---

[1]  Carol Chomsky. "Write First, Read Later," in *Childhood Education,* March 1971.

[2]  Debra was doing her practice teaching, and Rosemary was her field adviser in the master's degree program, at the University of New Hampshire.

| | |
|---|---|
| J L E | jewelry |
| F S P L | fishing pole |
| B K | bike |
| B T | boat |

When I saw Jeanette a week later, she spoke enthusiastically about her visit to Debra's class. "It's the naturalness of what the children were doing that appeals to me," she said. "They were really listening to the sounds they make when they said those words, they were working alone but also together on the problems, and they were using what information they had to figure out possible spellings. There was important learning going on; I think I'm going to try encouraging my children in that direction. It will be my little experiment."

Later in the year, pleased by the work of her children, Jeanette arranged a meeting for parents and teachers at her school, and she invited Debra Cheney and Carol Chomsky to make presentations, an event that, in retrospect, marked the end of the "little experiment" and the beginning of an established new approach to reading and writing in the Amidon first grade.

**"Talking" on Paper.** As if triggered by those seminal events, writing began to flourish as never before in Room 101 and has continued to flourish ever since. It's as though these children, freed from the burden of having to spell correctly, are discovering yet another medium through which to release and express their creative energies. Here is an example, a story written by Kevin, which originally appeared in book form—one sentence on each page and a drawing to go with each sentence. The reader will no doubt be grateful for the translation provided here.

## The Year Without a Santa Claus by Kevin

| | |
|---|---|
| I the ks yt md if | I think the kids won't mind if |
| I ks krisms | I cancel Christmas. |
| No toes | No toys! |
| Sad ksd krisms | Santa canceled Christmas. |
| The kes w sid | The kids were sad. |
| It ys nst krs | It is next Christmas. |
| Mi stokn | My stocking! |
| kok Dsn NKN NGB | Calling Dasher, Comet and Cupid. |
| M sms | Merry Christmas! |
| I love Ksms | I love Christmas. |
| Y ds it h to snow | Why does it have to snow |
| it Kms | at Christmas? |
| Y is gen n rid the | Why is green and red the |
| Kol krsms | color of Christmas? |
| is the s the | Is there such a thing |
| is fin rds | as flying reindeer? |

**Invented Spelling as Mental Activity.** To those of us who learned to read and spell years ago, such invented spelling can seem not only confusing but also off-putting. It can be hard for us to understand what the child is doing, and whether it's really worth doing. We need to try to get inside the child's head—even though that's impossible. One way to approach this impossible task is to recognize that once *we* know how to spell a word—the word *Christmas* for example—it's hard for us to think about the *sound* of that word without also thinking about the *look* of it. But the child doesn't know the look of it; he only knows the sound. I find that if I close my eyes and say the word *Christmas,* trying hard not to see it, I can more easily imagine what the children are struggling with, more easily understand their spellings, more easily understand the importance of what they are doing.

Perhaps at this point a brief definition of invented spelling might be useful. This is how I see it. *Invented spelling* is a technical term (used by the linguist Carol Chomsky, among others) in referring to a young child's efforts to write words from her own speech before she has learned the correct spellings of the words. It is the process that goes on in the child's head when she listens to the sounds in the words she wants to write and then writes whatever graphic symbols she knows, or can contrive, to represent those sounds. This is a mental process involving mental "inventions," the visible part being what appears on paper. The psychologist Piaget used the term *invented* in a similar way.

Having contrived this definition I must now admit that it's a bit too pure to account for the range of curiosities that occur when children cut loose with stories in invented spelling. To solve their spelling problems children seem to draw clues from many sources, some traceable, some not. Still, there are general patterns of linguistic development that show forth in children's writing patterns which suggest persistent inquiry, experimentation, and growth. The following samples of writing are meant to illustrate some of these patterns, as well as features more personal and idiosyncratic. The reader should bear in mind that these stories were originally written in book form, generally with one sentence to a page, usually an illustration on each page. Some readers may enjoy the challenge of trying to decipher a child's invented spellings *before* looking at the translation. Putting your hand (or a sheet of paper) over the translation will make it easier for you to carry on your struggle, while resisting the temptation to peek at the "answers." I hope that you will not become so engrossed in code cracking that you fail to notice what the children are writing about!

There is a general pattern of development that can be seen in children's early writing when they are encouraged to spell words the way they sound. At first, many children notice just the consonant sounds, maybe only the first consonant of a word. Even at this early stage some children pick up the correct spelling of common words such as *the*.

SP N THE F S    Snoopy in the firehouse

Gradually they become aware of more consonant sounds, at the ends of words and in the middle.

I OF THE HKE    One of the hockey

PLR GT HRT    players got hurt.

For many children awareness of vowel sounds comes still later, and the long vowel sounds seem easier to identify than the short ones, no doubt because the sound is the same as the name.

HAY R SAL THE BOT     They are sailing the boat.

HAY R AT THE BECH     They are at the beach.

Gradually children's ears become sensitive to the flow of sounds, and their spelling moves closer to standard forms.

IF YOU LIFE IN JAPAN YOU SLEP ON

THE FLOR AND YOU EAT ON THE FLOR TOO.

In their early writing children often seem to be using information from several sources:

- the sounds they hear in words (an auditory source), combined with the graphics they know or invent for representing those sounds;

- their memory (often garbled or inexact) of spellings they may have seen (a visual source);

- the correct spelling of a word that might be immediately available, perhaps from a friend more advanced in reading and writing (copying).

Often it's impossible to be sure which of these sources (or possibly a combination) a child used in arriving at a particular spelling, but it can be an interesting thing to speculate about. Douglas's story about Christmas and Rudolph seems to be a mix of these three sources.

KRISMIS IS SOONU WE HAFTR TO GO TO SKOOL.

KRIMIS IS 3 WEIKS AWAYE ON AER WAYE WE
SOR ROODOOF.

IT IS CHRISTMAS HE WAS SAD.

CHRISTMAS IS OVER WE MADE ROODOOF HAPPY.

WE ARE PLAYING ROODOOF WENT WITH US.

WE HAFTR TO GO IN MEREY KRIMIS.

THE END

At this early stage the teacher will often need the child to translate his own message—immediately, as the child may forget what he wrote. Even Jeanette with all her experience cannot read everything children write. In her classroom not all children are writing at the same time, so Jeanette usually is able to reach each child as he or she works. Imagine formalizing this activity and having 30 stories written all at the same time and handed in for translation. Impossible!

## Police by Marty

ETHEI R WZ

RBR I GD THE RW

There was a

robbery. I got the robber.

WE T THE RB

BK TO PE S

We took the robber

back to the police station–

DN SR N THE PE

down to the cellar in the
police station.

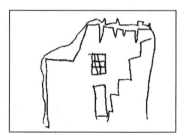

HE GR OF THE

PL SN AZ HS ADT

CS

The garage of the

police station has horses and

cars.

ETHEIR WZ ANR HRB

I C THE RB THE ND

There was another robbery.

I caught the robber. The end

Simon was just beginning to hear sounds in sequence. On page four he gave up the effort to complete his sentence, but when reading it later he remembered what he had intended to say. On page six he could not remember his fourth word and said, "I think it's *presents*," but Jeanette thinks he probably had a different word in mind when he was writing.

## *The Hanukkah Book  by Simon*

| p. 1 | THES IS THE | This is the |
| | HINEION BIOO | Hanukkah Book. |
| p. 2 | TOM TO GAT | Time to get |
| | THE TOSE | the toys. |
| p. 3 | I MEN OPING | I am opening |
| | THE PSZTS | the presents. |
| p. 4 | MI BIS R MAET | My brothers are mad |
| | KIS................... | because they didn't get toys. |
| p. 5 | ASE GAT BIRK | They got bikes. |
| p. 6 | I GOT TO SAS | I got two presents. |

Here's invented spelling combined with correct spelling. Luke was using words he recognized in his classroom. He found the word *morning* on a songsheet titled "Morning Has Broken." The word *making* was on a sign in the block corner.

## Christmas by Luke

| | |
|---|---|
| Stmtas Morning | Christmas morning. |
| It is Stmtas Morning | It is Christmas morning. |
| WE AARE PAEOLING | We are playing |
| WERU RU TIOES | with our toys. |
| THE LZ R MAKING | The elves are making |
| BUG CENDE KANZ | big candy canes. |

Children in the process of composing have many things to think about, and so they often do not spell inventively as well as they could if constrained to give spelling their full attention. Sometimes children become so absorbed in what they want to write that their spellings trip out almost like shorthand. To illustrate this point for me Jeanette one day asked Jerry to rewrite the text of his Animal Wish Book and to make any improvements in the spelling that he could. Here is a portion of Jerry's original text, then his improvements, then the translation.

| *THE ANAR WH BOOK* | *THE ANDIMLE WISH BOOK* | **The Animal Wish Book** |
|---|---|---|
| p. 1    wt wd lalaft | wat wad a lafnt | What would an elephant |
| wh for i no | wish for i on | wish for? I know, |
| mr gs | mr gras | more grass. |
| p. 2    wt a fth | wat wad a fish | What would a fish |
| w for the hl | wish for the hl | wish for? The whole |
| wid to be ohn | world to be oth | world to be ocean. |
| p. 3    hm ting ca | haoo mne ting can | How many things can |
| you wh fro | you wish for | you wish for? |

To begin to write by inventing spellings for words a child must have at least an intuitive awareness that the way people write words has something to do with the way they say them. Building on that basic understanding the child develops the ability to hear the component sounds of words: to hear, for example, what sound comes first, or last, in a word or syllable as he says the word, then to represent those sounds using graphic symbols (usually letters) arranged in order from first to last, which in English means from left to right across the page. These learnings involve complex neurological coordinations that link up seeing, hearing, and physical action, the matrix for which is the child's knowledge of the spoken language. Jeanette emphasizes the informal ways that these abilities develop:

- through the sheer enjoyment of talking and the use of speech for expression and communication;

- through responding to rhymes, alphabet games, and other forms of playfulness with words and sounds;

- through listening to quality literature and poetry and talking about what has been heard; and of course

- through the child's own creative expression in writing and drawing.

Enjoyment seems to be the key. If children enjoy language, they're likely to go on learning more about it and how to use it.

**Learning Correct Spellings.** As children are enjoying language, especially in its written form, they become more aware, visually and intellectually, of the patterns of English spelling and also of the irregularities that give English spelling its dubiously celebrated complexity. Through this unpressured approach to self-expression and communication, children quite naturally sneak up on correctness in spelling, getting better gradually, as is the way with most learning. Some interesting examples of "sneaking up" were produced by the Amidon class of 1993, in response to a series of quizzes that Jeanette gave, by special request of her principal.[1] The *same group* of twenty words was dictated to the children, first in October, then in

---

[1] Out of personal interest Principal Douglas Weinstock asked his first grade teachers to give this quiz to their children. Jeanette, normally opposed to testing children of this age, agreed. The word list was developed by a New Hampshire teacher, Mary Ellen Giacobbe, who had visited Jeanette's classroom many years before and was apparently intrigued by what she saw.

March, then in June. On each occasion Jeanette asked the children to make their best guess about how each word would be spelled. (Obviously, no special attention was given to these words during the course of the year.) The table on the next page shows representative examples of children's responses to seven of the twenty words in these quizzes.

Some points worth noticing:

- In October Charlie spelled words by putting down the initial sound followed by a random bunch of letters. By March he knew a great deal more.

- As the year progressed the children were able to identify more sounds and to represent them in spelling, even though incorrectly. Note, for example, Kevin's progress in spelling *doctor* and *yellow,* Bobby's progress in spelling *six,* and Susan's in spelling *view.*

- As the children's knowledge increased, their spelling errors become more "sensible"—for example, SICKS, YELLOE, ZEROE, QWIK, DOCTR, PIKAL, VYOU.

| | | SIX | DOCTOR | VIEW | YELLOW | ZERO | PICKLE | QUICK |
|---|---|---|---|---|---|---|---|---|
| **TOM** | **OCT** | SICS | DACR | VIVD | YEITTO | ZRO | PCAL | CIK |
| | **MAR** | SIZ | DOCDR | VUOOE | YELLEO | ZURO | PICL | CIK |
| | **JUNE** | SIX | DOCKER | VUOO | YWELLO | ZERO | PICK | QUICK |
| **EMILY** | **OCT** | SIS | DOCDIL | VOW | YOLLEW | ZERO | PICKOL | QUICKK |
| | **MAR** | SIX | DOCDR | VUOE | YELLOW | ZERO | PIKO | QUIK |
| | **JUNE** | SIX | DOCDER | VYOU | YELLOW | ZERO | PICL | QUIC |
| **BOBBY** | **OCT** | SIES | DACDR | VQUOW | YELLOW | SERO | PICEL | QUIK |
| | **MAR** | SICKS | DAKTR | VYOU | YILLOO | ZIRO | PIKL | KWIC |
| | **JUNE** | SIXS | DAKTOR | VUOW | YELLOW | ZERO | PIKAL | QWIK |
| **KEVIN** | **OCT** | SES | DITR | VEU | EELO | SERO | PCL | KWCIHICK |
| | **MAR** | SEGS | DGD | FOYOU | YLO | ZERO | PECTAL | KWICK |
| | **JUNE** | SIX | DOKDR | VAUE | YALO | ZEROE | PIKL | QICK |
| **SUSAN** | **OCT** | SAKS | DAKDR | VEV | EALO | ZERAO | PAKAI | KAK |
| | **MAR** | SICKS | DOCDR | VUEY | YELO | ZERO | PICL | QIK |
| | **JUNE** | SIX | DOCTR | VEYUE | YELLOE | ZEROE | PICL | QICK |
| **CHARLIE** | **OCT** | SDRHZY | DLYNRYZN | VUNARIH | YUNDRI | ZO | PEXNARUR | KGWERID |
| | **MAR** | SIX | DOTER | VYOU | YAILE | SEROW | PICKLE | QIEK |
| | **JUNE** | SIX | DOCTER | VYOU | YOLOW | ZAIRO | PICKILE | QUICK |

**Explosion into Writing.** Without spelling requirements to interfere, the children's expressive needs unfolded. Here are several
pages from a book by Mark.

## Things You Can Do by Mark

| | | |
|---|---|---|
| p. 1 | You can play owsid | You can play outside |
| | gams like run the | games like run the |
| | bais basbol trrakbol | bases, baseball, trackball, |
| | sading | skating. |
| p. 2 | You kian plae Hoke | You can play hockey |
| | like ties boys | like these boys. |
| p. 3 | Ties is a biskl ras | This is a bicycle race. |
| | If you go off the | If you go off the |
| | trrak you hfto chri | track you have to try |
| | to go throw the fire | to go through the fire. |
| p. 4 | You kin mak | You can make |
| | pabr sow flaks | paper snowflakes. |
| | All you hftodo is | All you have to do is |
| | take pes of pabr | take a piece of paper |
| | and fold it three | and fold it three |
| | tims in a trriagl | times in a triangle |
| | like tas | like this. |

The complete text of The Book About Rudolph, The Red-nosed Reindeer, by Joanie, which Rosemary referred to in Chapter 1, Jeanette's Classroom.

## THE BOOK A BOT ROODDOF THE RED NOOS RADR

| | | |
|---|---|---|
| p. 1 | Mommy I dont wont this noas | Mommy, I don't want this nose! |
| p. 2 | Fathr Rooddof dusit like his noas | Father, Rudolph doesn't like his nose. |
| | I doo no wut too doo | I do know what to do. |
| p. 3 | Fathr poot on a blak noas | Father put on a black nose. |
| p. 4 | I don't want this noas | I don't want this nose. |
| p. 5 | Thay wit to a radr game | They went to a reindeer game. |
| p. 6 | His noas fall off and thay | His nose fell off and they |
| | did not lat him play | did not let him play. |
| p. 7 | He ran away | He ran away. |
| p. 8 | He cam bak. Tay all wr hpee | He came back. They all were happy. |
| | The end | The end |

# A Book about Cats by Sally

|       |                                                                                 |                                                           |
|-------|---------------------------------------------------------------------------------|-----------------------------------------------------------|
| p. 1  | Cats dringk all the time. Thea bont stop.                                        | Cats drink all the time. They don't stop.                 |
| p. 2  | Thea allso pllye with sring—loots.                                              | They also play with string—lots!                          |
| p. 3  | Thea allso sleep on the rateeatr mor thne thea shood too.                        | They also sleep on the radiator more than they should too. |
| p. 4  | Well thea bont boothr you for a sekint bot aftr thea tak ovre the holl hous.     | Well, they don't bother you for a second, but after, they take over the whole house! |
| p. 5  | I allmost forgot its my brthday. I hope I get a cat.                             | I almost forgot. It's my birthday. I hope I get a cat.     |

| | | |
|---|---|---|
| p. 6 | I *bib*! I *bib*. | I did! I did! |
| p. 7 | I have to *feeb* my new cat. Here is yore lunch | I have to feed my new cat. Here is your lunch. |
| p. 8 | Theats wots a matr with tham. Thea have babys | That's what's the matter with them. They have babies. |
| | I *ket* andrsed it. | I can't understand it. |
| p. 9 | Cats have *babys* all the time | Cats have babies all the time. |
| | I *ges* all have to keep them | I guess I'll have to keep them. |
| p. 10 | Lets go for a wok cats. | Let's go for a walk, cats. |
| | The end | The end |

The first part of

## *When I Was Little  by Pamela*

I had a Wonnerful House. I Loved it. Me—my sister Hoos Name was Ellen Had our own Bedrooms. It was so Buettfull. One night my momy and Dady desided they were going to get a Divorse. A divorse is what you get wen your momy - Dady get made. One of them stays in the old House the other Mooves. When I got my Divorse Me and Ellen swich Houses. On school days we are at Moms On weekends we are AT Dads. Both houses were Buetiful. But Both Me and Ellen like the House ware Both our parints Lived at the same time together. That House was in the woods. Me and Ellen would ....

The opportunity and encouragement to write gives children an important outlet for some of their deepest feelings and a way of coping with situations that are hard for them to understand.

A note to a friend:


## To Sally


Do you like Pupcin[1] Sally

Wall last night at 8:30

Pupkin got hit By my bad

and mom hee got hit by

a car   We are sad

form Jennifer

and it is true

---

[1] "Pumpkin" is Jennifer's cat.

From the first four pages of

## *The Pain Book!!!  by Billy*

| | | |
|---|---|---|
| p. 1 | Yasterdae I wet to | Yesterday I went to |
| | the datisst. It wus | the dentist. It was |
| | prite mush pane | pretty much pain! |
| p. 2 | The dae bfor I wit | The day before I went |
| | to the datisst I wot | to the dentist I went |
| | to the doters. He gave | to the doctors. He gave |
| | me a shot It wus pane | me a shot. It was pain! |
| p. 3 | The dae bfore I wet | The day before I went |
| | to the doter I sprade | to the doctor I sprained |
| | my akl on the stip | my ankle on the step. |
| | It is pane | It is pain! |
| p. 4 | Sumtimse Miss Amidon | Sometimes Mrs. Amidon |
| | gats pane in hier eas | gets pain in her ears – |
| | gats pane ril pane. | gets pain, real pain. |
| | The chigrin do it | The children do it! |

When Billy wrote this book, his father was dying of cancer and was in great pain. For the "author page" of his book Billy dictated what he wanted and said: "I wrote this book because I think a lot of people have a lot of pain—and that's the truth." Billy's acceptance of his father's death was partly his seeing it as a release from pain.

**Book Publishing and Reading.**  I mentioned that these stories are generally written in the form of "books," and that many of these books get published by the Room 101 classroom "press." Book publishing has become something of a cottage industry in this room. Not all of the manuscripts get published, of course. Jeanette tells me that she takes a number of things into account in deciding whether or not to publish a child's work. Sometimes she feels a child really needs to publish for some special reason. Sometimes she decides against publishing because a child may have had enough attention for a while. Sometimes she has to take account of parental pride or, possibly, resentment. The reasons can get pretty complicated and can involve more than the quality of the work or the effort of the writer. Celeste, for example, was a prolific writer and very imaginative, and the children loved her books. They also knew that Jeanette wouldn't publish too many for one child. Sometimes the children tried to persuade her that Celeste had written something that simply had to be published. Her decision then, as always, reflected her sensitivity to the children and their needs.

Each year the children's published books, including a few titles from a previous year, plus a library of quality children's literature, become the principal reading fare of the classroom. As a consequence, basal readers and workbooks have virtually disappeared, and "reading groups" have proved unnecessary. Yet the children do learn to read, as well as or better than with Jeanette's earlier approach.

Clearly, the children's writing and the book publishing in particular are vital parts of this scene. The published version of a book is run off on a copier located in the hallway outside the classroom. Each child gets a copy of each book, so that personal libraries become quickly established and quickly grow. The published version contains the author's illustrations, plus the author's text, which an adult editor writes in *correct spelling* on each page—so that the book can be easily read by anyone who is interested. At the end of the book is the author's original text (showing original spellings) condensed onto a single page by the editor. There is also a title page and a page called "About the Author," which contains pertinent remarks, frequently supplied by the author.

The entire publishing process obviously requires a great deal of adult time. In the late '70s when her classes exceeded 25 children, Jeanette qualified for an aide. Later, with somewhat smaller classes, she relied on parents, on her student teacher, and, not infrequently, on special volunteers who contributed in a variety of ways to the life of the classroom. For at least 12 years Anne Perrino, the "class grandmother," came in one morning a week. A "class aunty," Elaine Levis, a retired high school English teacher, gave one morning a week to work with the children. Her after-action reports, detailed and perceptive, helped document in writing the life of the classroom. Gloria Kezerian, another "class aunty," who worked part-time at a local bank, helped the children with the computer. She also liked to listen to them read. Then Mora Owens, a high school senior who used to be in Jeanette's first grade, began coming in several times a week as part of her "community service work." All of these special helpers have contributed to the family atmosphere of the classroom.

To get a sense of the children's books in their published form, there is no substitute for looking at the real thing, which in this case begins with a one-page effort by Chris.

When Chris produced this picture and this "sentence," he had been in first grade for about three weeks. He could not read at all. He drew the picture first, then began writing, at the middle of the page— PLS—and so on to the right edge of the page. Then he moved to the top left and continued writing from left to right. When he had finished, Jeanette asked him what he had written, and he said: "Please don't touch my pumpkin or else it will bite you."

As adult eyes are accustomed to seeing words separated by spaces, Chris's sentence may become easier for us to read if we respace it:

PLS DT TICH M PCN

R S AT WL BT U

From this work we can see that Chris was hearing most of the consonant sounds, was hearing them in correct order, and was able to write them in correct order from left to right. We can also see that he was just beginning to notice and identify vowel sounds.

Apparently still hooked on pumpkins, Chris one month later produced his first book, a five-pager titled TH PTCN BRC (The Pumpkin Book).

THE WCH AS MD

TH W MD BCS HOWN AS OOFR

HOAN AS BAC

AN NT SDE AT TH SCRE VINGS TC OVR TH WRD

TH S FING T F WRD ANSDIT

The witch is mad.

The witch is mad because Halloween is over.

Halloween is back.

In nineteen seventy-eight the scary things took over the world.

The scary things turned the world inside out.

**Conditions for Development.** Regardless of what one thinks about the technical qualities of the writing, one thing seems clear: the children's efforts come from deep inside. It's as though the powers that these children used in learning to walk and talk are now being applied to the problem of learning to write and spell and read. Whereas at an earlier stage the children were trying to figure out how the spoken language operates, at this stage they are trying to figure out how the written language operates. At both stages the process reveals the active mind at work, and at both stages the children benefit enormously from a responsive human and material environment, an environment that surrounds them with encouragement for what they are trying to learn, an environment that provides helpful but nonthreatening feedback so that they can tell how well they're doing.

One might argue that the urge to learn to talk lies deeper and is more organic to growth than the urge to write. Maybe so. One might also say that children won't write, as these children write, without a teacher who puts her priorities in that direction. I'm sure this is so. Jeanette Amidon is passionately interested in children's development, particularly their language development, and she encourages this in many ways. But it is also true, paradoxically, that Jeanette's children write because they feel so free *not* to write. Writing is valued, but many other things are valued also. In this classroom there are many ways, equally legitimate, for children to express and develop their powers.

**A Letter to Parents.** In 1977, as this "new way of writing" became known in the Winn Brook School community, Jeanette recognized the need to help her children's parents, and even her fellow teachers, understand what she was doing and why. I offered to put together an interpretive piece in which I would try to explain to others what I was then coming to understand myself, how expressive writing and invented spelling are related to a child's intellectual development, including development into literacy. I did this in the form of a letter to the parents of children in Jeanette's classroom. The first part of the letter featured examples and commentary similar to what has just been presented in this book. In the final part I considered hypothetical questions a skeptical adult might ask about invented spelling in the classroom. Here is that final section.

## *Won't children get the wrong idea about spelling if we encourage them to be inventive with it? After all, a word is either correctly spelled or it's not.*

There is a creative side to invented spelling, but creativity is not the objective. The purpose, rather, is to encourage the child to listen to the sounds he hears when he says a word and to write symbols representing those sounds. He is working on his own awareness. An important feature of a child's writing "inventions" is the way they evolve toward correctness as he becomes more aware of sounds and spellings and the formation of letters. But the evolution rarely proceeds in a straight line. In a child's early writing we can observe a good deal of to-ing and fro-ing, fading in and fading out, as the child uses information and skills not yet firmly under control. It is not unusual for him to misspell the same word two or three different ways in the same story, for example, or to form the same letter two or three different ways. We need to bear in mind that when everything is new and when nothing has become automatic, there is a lot for a child to think about all at once. Some adults worry about a child's inconsistencies and "reversals," which are a normal feature of learning at this stage and which gradually fade if the child is given full opportunity to focus inwardly and sort out what he needs to know. The danger is in pushing a child, or making him feel a failure, or, worse yet, classifying him as a misfit or "problem." Such treatment makes him anxious, and anxiety, more than anything else, walls him off from that vital contact with his own awareness.

### Aren't children learning incorrect spellings that will have to be unlearned later?

The children are under no illusions about correctness. They know they're not spelling the way adults do. They see correct spellings all around the room, and their own books are edited (by adults) into correct spelling before they are published—but with the original spellings included at the back of each book. As children master the basic coordinations and become more confident in their ability to "sound out" words, they become more interested in correct spellings. Then is the time to introduce various games and activities that help develop the visual memory. Such activities are available in this classroom, and many children begin to find them interesting, particularly toward the end of the first grade year, when their reading skills are more fully developed. A child's invented spelling gives us a window on her awareness: she is giving us some visible signals of what is going on in her head. In the early stages it is not correctness that is important to the teacher but a child's progress toward correctness. A child who writes SANA IS SIK (Santa is sick) is further along than a child who writes ST Z SK, and that child is further along than one who writes S K. What a child knows and can do is just as important, indeed more important, to the teacher than what she doesn't know and cannot do. When we encourage a child to spell words the way they sound to her, we encourage her to open that window. The alternative is to keep the window shut, by not encouraging children to write and by insisting on correctness—which is what happens in many classrooms.

### But for years, children have been learning without the benefit of invented spelling.

Most children pick up these vital coordinations (the ability to read and write unfamiliar words by sounding them out) from traditional methods of instruction in which correctness is emphasized from the beginning. But many children do not, and they become casualties—

our remedial readers, "language disability" cases, and functional illiterates. We have other casualties too—the children who are turned off school because their schooling has been little more than a succession of skill exercises divorced from life and experience. Skills are seldom well-learned apart from situations that require their use. Most of us learn best by doing, and in the process our minds are exercised and expanded. And what's more, like Jeanette's children, we find joy in the doing.

### *Aren't there more direct ways of helping children learn to "sound out" words?*

Yes, of course, but the most directive methods seem to make the children feel passive and dependent, whereas they could be feeling active and responsible. It's an inherently stressful trip too, with some children doing well and some doing poorly and competition being almost unavoidable. In the grip of anxiety, frustration, and failure many children lose touch with their own awareness and recklessly search for ways to give the teacher the answers they think she wants. These children become surefire candidates for remedial reading. In situations where young children are in control of their own expressive activities, indeed where they have a significant part in shaping what happens during the school day, they are constantly revealing what they can do without the teacher's help and also the kind of help they need her for. The sensitive and experienced teacher knows how to read these signals. There need be no failure, no frustration, and, I predict, much less "remedial reading" than we have now in most schools. I am not implying that all children will be fully functioning readers by the end of first grade. Some will not. I am implying that in this kind of supportive environment all children will move forward in their learning and will have a keen sense of their own travel. Our job as teachers and parents is to sustain that kind of environment and that momentum.

# 3

# A LOT ON THEIR MINDS

*– a closer look at the work of the children –*

The previous chapter emphasized invented spelling. It is true that Jeanette's children are often thinking about how to spell certain words, but this thinking is usually incidental to the expression of ideas. The children's work is a constant reminder that their heads are humming with serious concerns, concerns that compel their attention and spur them to expressive activity. In recent years it has become fashionable in school circles to talk about the importance of "teaching children how to think." The phrase seems to imply that children are not very good at thinking until someone teaches them how to do it. Yet a day spent in Jeanette's classroom enables the well-tuned observer to gather persuasive evidence that thinking comes as naturally to young children as wiggling and talking. (Indeed, the thinking seems to increase in proportion to the wiggling and talking!) The point is that adults must make the effort to get on children's wavelengths in order to begin to understand their intellectual life and to appreciate its richness and vitality. Children are often not very good at getting on our wavelengths, are easily confused by our language, can easily be made to appear stupid. In her talks with teachers, Rosemary often spoke of "paying attention to what the child is paying attention to." Those who have learned to do this, whether as teachers, as parents, or simply as friends, have discovered much about the vibrant intellectual life of children. In the process they may have found their own lives enriched.

In going through the children's books published during a single year I decided to pay special attention to *what* these individuals were writing about—their ideas, interests, and concerns—and from this overview I made a list of what I found. Here is my list:

- exploring personal feelings—joy, worry, anger loneliness, jealousy, fear, love, grief

- exploring nature

- exploring what adults do

- exploring how things work

- telling how to do something or how to make something

- rehearsing things known and understood

- wondering about things unknown and mysterious

- expressing humor

- investigating connections and relationships

- exploring ways to express and communicate ideas

- exploring the skills of reading, writing, and spelling

- exploring words and the uses of language

- exploring alternatives to language (e.g., art)

- solving problems (of many different kinds)

- coping with personal adversity—pain, grief, separation

In the following samples of the children's writing I think the attentive and thoughtful reader will find evidence of much activity of thought, as suggested by the above list. The task of selecting the samples was formidable indeed. As I sat in the middle of the basement floor, surrounded by a sea of children's books, I realized that no samples can be truly representative. I also realized, once again, how much, and at the same time how little, a book reveals about the child who wrote it—a keyhole glimpse, at best, of the individual at a particular moment. What I finally decided upon was a small sampling of work chosen, not randomly, but—I would prefer to say—idiosyncratically, as the brief Introduction to each will suggest.

---

**Josh.** While blocks for building and construction are considered standard equipment for children's play in preschool, and probably in most kindergartens, they are not infrequently regarded by parents of first graders and, regrettably, by many first grade teachers, as "toys" these older children should have outgrown. For a variety of good reasons blocks remain as standard equipment in Jeanette Amidon's first grade classroom.

Josh was particularly interested in how things work. Many of his drawings and some of his books were about how things are built and how they go together. (Not surprisingly, Josh could often be found in the block corner!) One of his books was titled The Cinstrasin (The Construction). In doing this book Josh drew his pictures using colored felt pens. The original pages, reduced in size, appear here as rectangular boxes and are numbered to indicate the original sequence. To help the reader, translations of the invented spelling have also been added.

The men are constructing and they are trying to finish it.

He has fixed the fuse and he is testing the automatic night safe and it works.

The fuse is broken and the man is trying to fix it.

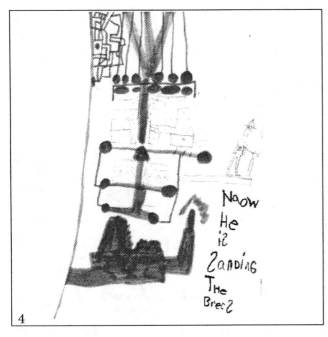

Now he is sending the bricks.

Now the bricks are down.

Now they are putting the bricks.

Now they are finishing the walls.

8

Now he is finishing up.

9

Now the building is just
about finished.

Now

Holiday Inn

**Prasit.** Prasit came to the United States from Thailand. At the beginning of first grade he could not speak a word of English. By the end of the year he could carry on an easy conversation and could read and write. He loved to draw and tell stories of violent action. In this book, his second to be published by the Room 101 Press, he first drew the pictures, then dictated the story to Charlene Gavrilles, Jeanette's student teacher.

The good soldier is coming to the castle. The man will pull the drawbridge down for him.

The soldier is saluting the King.

The soldier is getting ready to fight.

This is the good soldier.

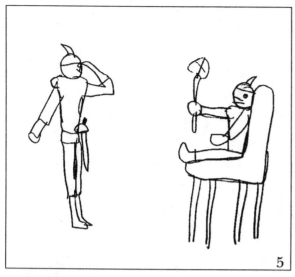

The king tells the good soldier to go help the other good soldiers.

He is leaving the castle; ready to fight.

The good soldier was wounded by the sword of the bad soldier.

The good soldier is going to help the other good soldier.

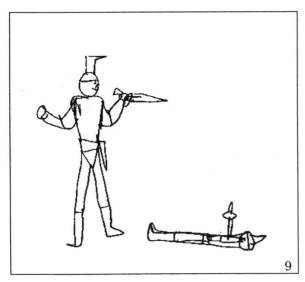

The bad soldier killed the good soldier.

The good soldier is helping his friend. He is shooting an arrow at the bad soldier.

The bad soldier finds his friend and he is crying *because* he is dead.

The good soldier is taking his friend back to the castle.

He is going into the castle with his friend.

He is opening the door.

The soldier brings his friend in front of the King and salutes him.

The soldier buried his friend. He and the King are visiting him. They are both crying.

On toward March Prasit was writing stories on his own. By that time Jeanette had grown weary of guns, swords, and violence (a theme that had become contagious amongst one group of boys), so one day, in exasperation, she called a class meeting and decreed:

"No more guns!

"No more killings!

"Write about anything you like, but *no more violence!*"

So, Prasit produced his version of The Gingerbread Boy, in which an eagle almost gets bashed by the little old man and the gingerbread boy finally gets eaten by a fierce crocodile. Pretty hard for teacher to quarrel with violence when it comes from such a legitimate source!

Prasit's artwork in this later book has a slap-dash quality about it, so unlike the elegant dramatic action of his drawings in the The Soldiers Book. It's as though he was reveling in his ability to speak and write English. In his first book, words were subordinate to drawings. In the later book, drawings became subordinate to words. Or (as Rosemary points out to me) it might just be that Prasit preferred drawing soldiers to gingerbread boys. His "little old man working in the garden" looks more like a soldier than a farmer!

Here are several pages from The Gingerbread Boy.

1 Day The old woman made The gingerbread boy

The little old man was working in the garden He saw the gingerbread boy

Hi Do not go

2

The eagle gat the gingerbreadd Boy in The Cave

3

THE OLD man TRIED TO Kill The eagle

4

TheGingerBread Boy
ran To The hen house

5

the GingerBreadd Boy in
The Bot Boat

6

The GingerBreadd Boy Boy
Saw The STaue

7

THe CrocoDiole eat the
GingerBreadd Boy   THE EnD

8

**Celeste.** Celeste was one of those children—every first grade seems to have two or three—for whom reading and writing come easily, seemingly without struggle. During the course of the year she wrote many books, and a fair number were published. The children looked forward to the publishing of her books because they liked to read them, and Celeste's outpourings could have monopolized the Room 101 Press, if Jeanette had allowed it (which she didn't, of course).

In one of her early books, written in October, Celeste wrote about herself. She called it My Celeste Book. Here is the original version.

(The photograph was taken by Jeanette. Such photos can mean a lot to the children and are put to use in various ways which, to Jeanette, justify the expense. From time to time parents also take photographs, which frequently turn out to have classroom use.)

TO DAY I AM AT A PATEING CLAS WENDY IS NOT IN IT

4

NOW I AM IN THE BLOCK AREA

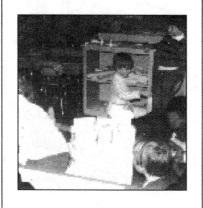

5

THEN KIM COMS OVR

Hi Kim

6

Celeste liked to make up stories about the adventures of animals. Usually she did her illustrations first, then wrote the story to go with the pictures. In May she wrote a book titled The Pigs. Here is the original version.

The pig's mud tub is fun for the pig kid's. Thar is Leny Rosy dugy, Sisy and Andy. Mama is eating a lot. It is hr diete. She is fat! The kids jump in the mud one by one all day.

The kids got ice cream cones. Dugy's ice cream cone fell in the mud. Sisy dos not like strawberry ice cream but she has to eat it.

The pigs had mud pies for diner. Thy all love mud pis. Mama Pig made butterfly cake for dusrt. Yum yum said Sisy. Mama Pig ate the leftovers.

It is Sisy birthday. Sisy got a mud pie and some old vegeables. We wood say yuk but Sisy ses ym.

**Sally.**   Sally also liked to write about animals but in a more personal way, based (obviously) on some personal experiences. Horses were a favorite topic. If you have not yet accepted the challenge of trying to read a child's invented spelling, a fresh opportunity has arrived!

We grownups sometimes forget what a child's eye view of the world must be like. Imagine the challenge of trying to mount a horse when you're only six. Imagine how you must feel once you're up there.

FORTH THing is to stat woking THe Hors.

4

FITH THing You cen start troting. THe end.

trne →

5

GOODY GOODY

6

ABOUt THe AtHr SALLY is AGOOd AtHre OF menee BOOK'S ASPeSHALeX Hors BOOK'S We Are LOOKING FORWRd to HEr NeXt BOOK We hoPe You inLoyd tHis BOOK OF Hers tHe end.

7

**Kim.** Isolated samples of children's writing (such as those we have been looking at) can help us form impressions of the classroom, the children, and the quality of work. But such samples tell us almost nothing about the development of one child's work during the course of a year. A closer look at such development may be of interest to many readers—bearing in mind that no two children develop in the same way or at the same rate. The next seven books show the development of Kim's writing. Her first book was a collection of fifteen felt pen drawings produced during a ten-day period. At that time Kim did not know any sound-letter relationships and had no grasp of the reading or writing process. Yet the advanced development of her artwork indicated to Jeanette that she probably was ready to begin the process of relating speech to writing. As Kim drew her pictures, she dictated a "story" about each one, and Jeanette wrote down what she said. Here are several pages from that joyful first book.

These are all twins. They are picking flowers.

They are in their dresses one by one.

She's on a boat.

They're outside decorating a vase for their mother.

In October Kim produced her second book, Witches and Ghosts, which contained her first attempt at writing—a mix of her own invented spellings and several correct spellings. She probably got the correct spelling of the word *ghost* from one of her special friends, Rhian and Meredith, who at that time were much further along with their writing and reading. Jeanette observed that Kim learned a lot from these two friends. In fact, she has a tape recording of Meredith helping Kim with the sounds of letters.

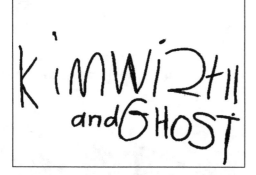

In this early part of the year Kim, unlike many of the children, went through a period when she was not ready to take the risk of spelling words the way they sound. She insisted on getting correct spellings, often from her friends or from a nearby adult. One reason for this insistence, Jeanette believes, was Kim's strong desire to emulate her two best friends. As a result she tended to write just those words she knew how to spell or thought she knew how to spell. Her first written sentences were quite stereotyped, as in About Home, written in November. Here are several pages, and the complete original text, from that book.

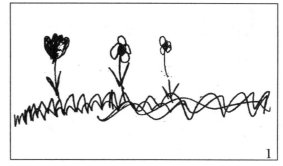

I *see* the flowr and raning and roz.

I *see* the sun.

I *see* a bot.

I *see* the stam of the Flwr.

I am hp (I am happy).

By December Kim was becoming more adventurous in using words she didn't know how to spell, more willing to spell them the way they sounded to her, not worrying about correctness. It's interesting to note how competently she was sequencing her ideas, giving one idea to each page.

Kim did not do a title page for this six-page book about Christmas and Hanukkah. Incidentally, do you remember what it feels like to sit at a big table when you're really small? Or stretch out on a triple-decker bed? Read on.

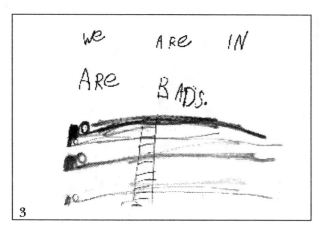

It is the first day of Hannukah.

The stockings are out.

We are in our beds.

It is breakfast.

In March Kim wrote a book about her after-school adventures. She called it The Jnastits and Bala Book (The Gymnastics and Ballet Book).

The Gymnastics and Ballet Book by Kim

I am going to gymnastics and after I am going to ballet.

I am at gymnastics. We do things with bars.

I am changing in the changing room.

I have some fun at gymnastics on the bars.

I am going to the horse bars now.

It is time to go to ballet.

I am walking to ballet now.

I am at ballet now.

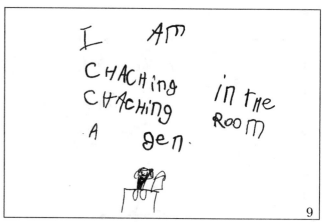

I am changing in the changing room again.

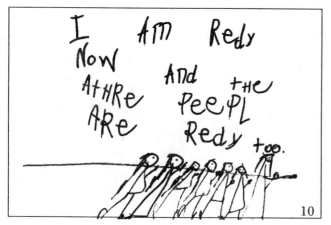

I am ready now and the other people are ready, too.

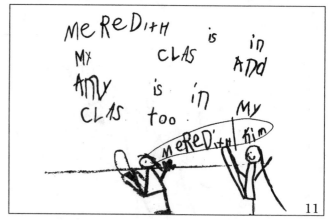

Meredith is in my class and Amy is in my class, too.

Mrs. O'Brien said Kim and Meredith are
the best.

Mrs. O'Brien is mad at Amy and Debby.

Mrs. O'Brien is giving Amy and Debby
a little medal.

I am going home. Meredith is going to my
home, too.

Meredith and me are getting some hot cocoa.

We are sleeping now.

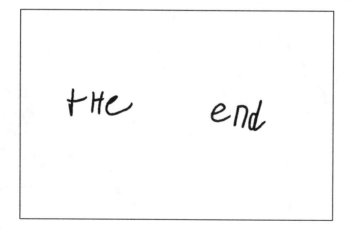

With many children the quality of their illustrations seems to improve with the quality of their writing. With others the illustrations take a back seat to writing, probably because the new process is so engrossing. This was the case with Kim: as she became more skillful with writing, she paid less attention to illustrating. In her last book of the year, written in late May, she scribbled illustrations on the first several pages, then dropped them entirely as she rushed her final messages onto paper.

Another interesting feature of Kim's writing is the "sensible errors" that occur on almost every page. Her misspellings reveal a thoughtful mind at work as she is continuing to sort out the complex patterns of English spelling.

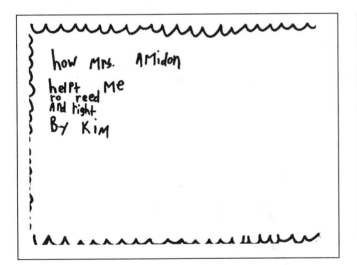

My      Mother      drovve      Me.
to      School         to      dAr.

SAw   Mrs.   AMidoN   one   girl.
Too   And   her   TALM   WAS   Meredith.

I    PlAI    With    Meredith
AND    Mrs.    AMidon   colld
ME

She      Wonid     Me      to      feed
So         I           did

I WASint very good.
I I terighd She sed
I WAS good

6

And We Went to
lunch And had dzert
And CAM back

7

And     CAM     foMe .
And     Week s     Went .
By     And     I StArtiD
to     Be     A good reedeh.

8

And     I     WAS     A good
reeder     And     Now     I
hAftoo     lern     to     right

9

And     I     row t     A
Book     Apowt     how
MrS.     A Midon     helPt
Me

10

RoBin     WAS     Mx     Secint
helPeh.

11

It     WAS     A     WeeKend -
We     Went     to     inglin D

12

And     We     CAM     bAcK.



the     End

13

What refreshing honesty in Kim's title, How Mrs. Amidon Helpt Me to Reed and Right. Not how Mrs. A. taught, not how she learned, but how she helpt her. No doubt about who was in charge of the enterprise, and no doubt about sharing credit for the achievement. Jeanette was intrigued by Kim's reference to "reed and right," as though "reed" occurred first, which it did not. So she asked Kim about this. "Oh no," Kim said, "I learned to write first, but I wanted to say read and write."

**Everybody.** Things the children write about in their books often seem quite unrelated to anything happening in school. But sometimes a school activity inspires writing, occasionally lots of it. This happened with the Camelot play, which more or less dominated the life of the classroom for about six weeks during the spring of this particular year, and which came about in a rather roundabout way. One of the high school teachers, having heard about the writing that was going on in the first grade, invited Jeanette's children to display some of their books in the corridor showcase at the high school. ("Your children's books might stimulate my 11th graders to write," she said.) Subsequently the 11th graders did some writing of their own, and their "books" were shared with the first grade.

An offshoot of this exchange (and of Mrs. Amidon's class giving a musical performance) was another invitation, for the first graders to put on a play for the 11th graders. It was to be the first graders' version of King Arthur and the Knights of the Round Table. (The older students had been studying the Arthurian legend as related to ideas of *power*–"might for right," "might makes right," etc.) One of the first grade mothers, with theater experience in her background, agreed to help the children develop the play. It turned out that the characters and plot unfolded over a period of at least six weeks, as the children heard the various King Arthur stories and discussed their own ideas about power.

On the night I saw the play (it was performed for several different audiences, and it came out differently each time), there was no mistaking whose play it was, for gathered about the Round Table were such illustrious characters as King Arthur, Queen Guinevere, Sir Lancelot, and Merlin, of course, but also Robin Hood, Superman, and Wonder Woman! Then there were George Washington, Martin Luther King Jr., Jimmy Carter, and Queen Elizabeth. And Moses (as a substitute for God, who was also proposed, then voted down— "because if we had Him, we wouldn't need anybody else!") and Maria (from *The Sound of Music*—"she was a mother to all those children and she was boss!"). And rounding out the cast were Mr. Blaney, the principal, and Mrs. Amidon.

The Camelot adventure stimulated a great deal of writing in the first grade, sooner or later nearly every child becoming involved. Again, as might be expected, the children wrote with characteristic individuality, as the following samples suggest.

Superman was losing at first. But now he is winning.

In Mark's book, Superman Wins Over Sir Lancelot, there was a brief moment when the outcome was in doubt.

In The Camelot Book, Josh (block builder and author of The Constrasin Book) was still trying to figure out how things work. Here he seemed to be tackling a problem in medieval fortification!

They are pulling the rock up.

In Kim's The Pretend Camelot Book, Guinevere was dealing with a less glamorous domestic problem.

Guinevere is sewing with her
sewing machine.

Alicia wrote Camelot—A Place Where Things Happen.

I am scared. I do not want to
marry the King.

Camelot had its special days too. Roberta wrote a book titled April Fools in Camelot.

March 27 in Camelot—Everyone was thinking of a riddle. King Arthur had a funny one.

King Arthur and the people are making laws.

Even in those days there were forces of darkness and, happily, of light. These are three scenes from Mickey's The Camelot Book.

Sir Lancelot rips the laws up.

"I am coming to stop you, Sir Lancelot," said George Washington.

**John.** John was the youngest child in the first grade. He could not read at all at the beginning of the year, but he loved to draw and he had an unusually lively imagination and inventive turn of mind. These qualities shone through in his pictures and stories. He also had a tendency to write letters backwards. Almost all children show some such tendency toward "reversals" when they're first learning to write. Jeanette did not consider him a "problem child" or "problem learner," and he did not receive any special "corrective" help during the year. He made slow but steady progress throughout the year and was reading quite well by year-end.

John brought a photograph of himself to school, cut out his face with a pair of scissors, and produced this.

John did this autobiographical book during the first week of school.

1

I'm in Mom's hands.

2

I'm cute.

3

Baby John.

4

(Jeanette asked John about the unidentified little girl in this picture. He said, "Oh, I forgot, I don't have a sister!")

John took to fairy tales of all sorts, especially *The Wizard of Oz*. The first time (so I'm told) that he went into the boys' lavatory, a room with gleaming ceramic walls, he threw back his arms rapturously and exclaimed, "Emerald City!" John's second book, written in September, featured Dorothy and the Wizard. The book began with Dorothy viewing the approaching tornado and shouting, "Oh, no!"

He then continued through various adventures including . . .

We're off to see the wizard, the wonderful wizard.

and finished up with a picture of Dorothy saying . . .

Good to be home.

In November John produced a book about the Three Stooges. Here are several scenes.

Larry, Curly, and Moe

You hit me.

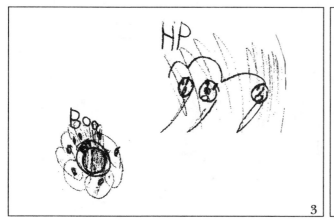

Boo                    Help

You look funny.

You don't spit at a girlie.

You too, Toots!

Goodnight.
Sleep tight.

One of John's favorite people was Farrah Fawcett
Majors, and he wrote a book about her adventures.
The book included this page . . .

Farrah Fawcett

and this one.

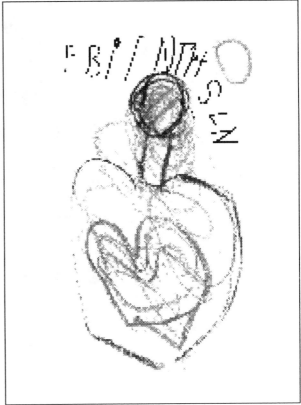

Farrah in the cyclone

Toward the end of the year John's artwork seemed to develop quite dramatically. One day in April he scratched off four or five pictures like these.

No no Rabbit

A Boy on a Skate Board

Humpty Dumpty

Jeanette admired these artistic efforts and asked John if he would like to do more pictures. Within about three days he had produced an impressive collection, which included . . .

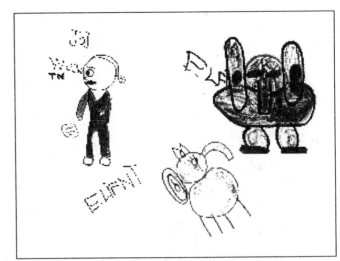

George Washington

Elephant

Elephant

Red Sox

A Boy Praying

Japanese Lady

Superman

Angel

Me!!!!

Late in the year John wrote Snow White and the Seven Dwarfs. It
was his last published book before going into second grade.

One day worked and worked a little girl.

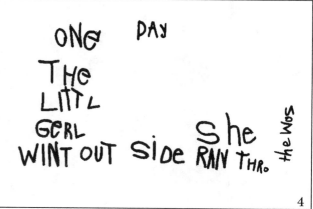

One day the queen said, Mirror Mirror on the wall.

One day the little girl went outside. She ran
through the woods.

Look, a little cottage.

She went in it.

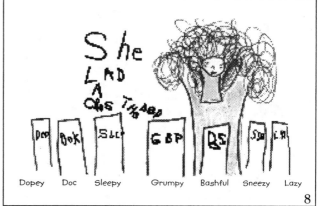

She laid across the bed.

(Unable to remember the seventh dwarf's name, John made one up.)

Dwarfs! Yes.

They went to work.

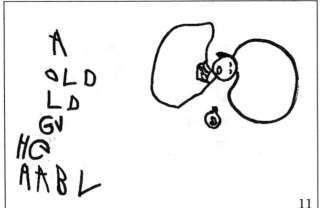

A old lady gave her a apple.

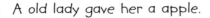

You saved me.

By springtime many of the children had become interested in keeping personal diaries, which they called their "journals" (very confidential, of course, and never published). For me a page from John's journal serves as a fitting close to the children's work.[1]

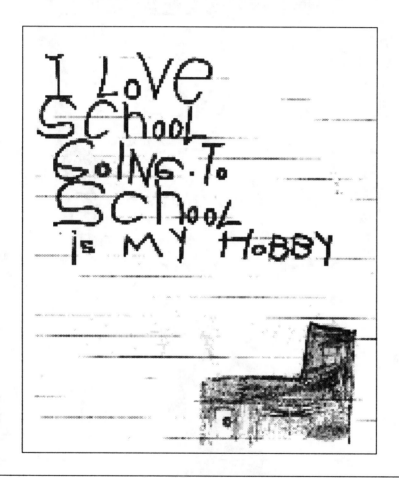

---

[1] Permission to use this personal journal page was granted by the author.

# CHEERING SECTION

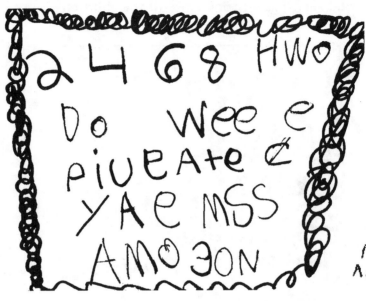

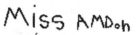

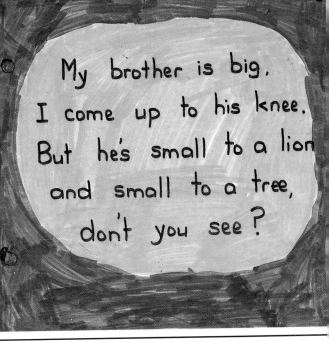

My brother is big.
I come up to his knee.
But he's small to a lion
and small to a tree,
don't you see?

Talk to the small mouse—
"Hi mouse, want to play?
want to race to the tree?
or stay?

I can run, run fast. I go!

What a pet!

Look out cat, here I come!

I Like

by Yukiko

I Like

Written and Illustrated by Yukiko
Edited by Donna La Roche

Published by the Room 160 Press    Nov. 1996

This is Quebec. This is    Castle.
2.

This is Mount Rainier. My family
Went to Mount Rainier. It is so
beautiful.    1.

I like Monument Valley. Monument
Valley is so beautiful!
2.

This is the church. The church is
so beautiful!    3.

This is Niagra Falls!
4.

This is earth. I like earth!
5.

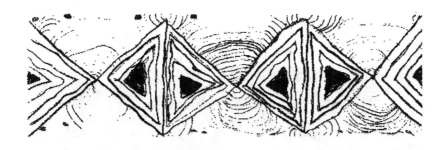

Dear Mrs. Amidon:

You r the *bst* teechr

in the wrld and I hop you nevr dy.

Yor frend Beth

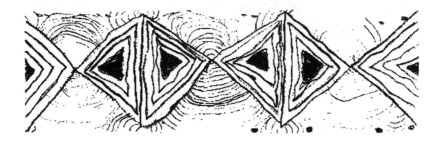

# 4

# THE LARGER PICTURE

*– we talk with Jeanette about children, learning, and teaching –*

In the introduction I said that there are things we can learn from our good teachers, if we can find ways of "tuning in to what they know, intuitively if not consciously, at the deeper levels of their craft." We have been attempting this "tuning in," first through a report of a visit to the classroom, then through a presentation of samples of the children's writing. Now it is time to talk with the teacher.

Rosemary, Jeanette, and I have been talking for many years, mostly in code, as is the way among friends. We seldom bother to elaborate the ins and outs of ideas that represent our common bonds, and in the classroom, complex messages sometimes pass in a knowing glance or an appreciative smile. This book calls for a different way of talking. Those complex messages, and simpler ones too, need to come forth in words available to all. But how do we break out of the code, and how do we put glances and smiles on paper?

As a start I decided to use the tape recorder. On three separate occasions we recorded our conversations about children, learning, and teaching, especially the learning and teaching in Jeanette's classroom. After each session I listened to the tapes and transcribed much of what I heard. The resulting documents were not exactly what any of us would have dared inflict on others, even our forgiving friends, so editing seemed essential. The editing revealed a need for additional input as we became aware of topics treated too lightly, or too obscurely, or not treated at all. Numerous short conversations followed, providing additional words and ideas for the text. My task was simplified enormously, and joyously, by Jeanette, who, when asked a general question, always responded in the specific, by talking about her children. Although Rosemary and I make our contributions, this is clearly Jeanette's story.

The final editing of the discussions yielded a version that we risked sharing with a close friend who, having read it, remarked, "But teachers don't talk like that." "Of course not," one of us replied, "but if we could, this is how we'd say it."

Each discussion is prefaced by a brief introduction.

*David, Jeanette, and Rosemary*

# DISCUSSION 1

*– we talk about curriculum –*

**Introduction.** *Curriculum* is a familiar word around schools. In the broad sense it's what happens there or more accurately, perhaps, what is supposed to happen. In my frequent visits to schools during the past thirty years, I have often asked teachers and administrators about their curriculum. Generally the answers go something like this: "We use Scott Foresman for reading and Addison Wesley for math," or "We're doing PSSC physics," or "We follow the school system syllabus." The common denominator of these and similar answers is that the curriculum is something ready-made—feel-able, see-able, usually name-able, put together by certain adults (usually "experts"), generally (but not always) adults other than the classroom teacher. The curriculum, so conceived, is something the children are expected to go through or be taken through, and from which they are expected to learn all that they're supposed to learn.

Sometimes (but not often) when I've inquired about curriculum, I've received quite different answers. One teacher replied, quite honestly, "I don't know yet. I'll be able to tell you when the year's over." One of her favorite ways of starting the school year was in a completely empty room—except for herself and the children. "We go from there," she said. A friend of mine in the Midwest took a more cautious but equally nontraditional approach. He taught ninth grade social studies in an inner-city school, one of those four-tiered chicken coop buildings erected in the 1890s. I visited his classroom in the fall of 1967, just after a "long hot summer" of racial unrest and violence.

The school principal showed me his collection of recently confiscated knives, and while I was visiting my friend upstairs, a pistol shot resounded downstairs. My friend's students were busy writing, using the textbook required by the school system. The book was a history of their city and told of its beautiful streets, parks, museums, and concert halls, and it told about its law courts and explained how the system of justice works or is supposed to work. "But it doesn't work that way for them," my friend explained to me. "Many of them have had brushes with the law, and some of them have brothers, and even fathers, in jail. As for the beautiful streets and parks and museums, well, all they can see from their homes is litter and broken glass." So what were the students writing? They were *rewriting* the text—they were "telling it like it is," the way they saw it, the way they knew it to be. After school I went with my friend to his apartment for a chat, and we talked about the problem of reaching the children that so many people regard as unreachable. One of his comments I will never forget. "What it takes," he said, "is a group of people, adults and kids, doing things together that really matter—to all of them."

I suspect that learners of any age, in any climate, are not really reached unless they are doing things that matter to them. I have always sensed this kind of involvement in Jeanette's classroom, where the curriculum *emerges* from work that is engrossing and important to all those involved, and so, for our first discussion, I wanted to get Jeanette talking about this kind of curriculum, to get her to describe, in words, things that she rarely has need to describe, because they are implicit in what she does.

# All Kinds of Celebrations–and Sad Times Too

D On our frequent visits to your apartment, Jeanette, you never fail to entertain us with the latest samples of the children's writing. During the past three years their work has given us so many things to think about, so many laughs, so much inspiration. I suppose that one way to get this discussion started would be with a simple question: how do you get children to write like that? But I know that question is too simple. It seems to imply that you have a certain method for teaching children to write, and that writing is separate from the rest of what's happening in your room. We know that's not true. The writing is one of the things that emerges from the atmosphere of the room.

J It's not that I have that atmosphere so that writing will emerge. It's that I believe in that kind of atmosphere and want it for lots of reasons, and the writing is one of the things that comes from it. I don't have blocks in my classroom so that children will write, and I don't let them talk and draw so that they'll write. I think that block building, drawing, and talking are important even if they don't lead to writing. I'm trying to give the children a life in the classroom, a happy life that's as natural as possible in such a setting, in which all kinds of learning can take place—and I mean that very broadly—a life in which all kinds of celebrations and happy times are shared, and sad times too. School is the children's life, and it's my life, a big part of my life. If I have to spend that many hours a day in something that's not living, so that I have to go home and start living after five o'clock and on weekends, there's something seriously wrong. I feel the same way about the children. They shouldn't have to wait until Saturday and Sunday to live. School consumes a great many hours of their waking day, and in the winter it's practically all of the time that they're not either eating or sleeping. My classroom is there for learning, but it's

> *they shouldn't
> have to wait until
> Saturday or
> Sunday to live*

learning in a very broad sense—about what life is, what people are like, what it's like to learn about the natural world and the world of books and all the things there are in life.

|D| I've always assumed that most six-year-olds, in our society at least, come to school expecting to be taught to read and write, expecting that the 3Rs will be the principal business.

|J| I think my children are sometimes thinking about reading and writing, but that's their agenda from home and from the community. They know that, "Oh yeah, in first grade I'm going to learn to read and write," but when they come into the room and see the blocks, the easels and paints, the glue and the toilet paper rolls, the paper and the colored felt pens, and all the costumes in the prop box, they forget all about what they're "supposed" to learn. Reading and writing may be in the back of their minds, but these activities are in the front. It's the same with me. Reading and writing are in the back of my mind, not in the front where they would dictate what we do every day. For me it's a combination of noticing what the children do in activities that they find genuinely engrossing and noticing how reading and writing fit in with those activities. And they do seem to fit in.

> *noticing what the children do in activities that they find genuinely engrossing and noticing how reading and writing fit in with those activities*

|D| Most teachers are accustomed to having a written-down curriculum, something that helps them know in advance what's going to happen each day or week, either because they've determined it or because somebody else has determined it for them. You don't follow such a curriculum. I think many teachers might wonder how you keep the children busy learning what they're supposed to learn.

|J| It just never occurs to me to wonder how I'm going to keep the children busy. It always occurs to me, "Gosh, how am I going to give them enough time for what they want to do and

have time for music and art and time for reading *Charlie and the Chocolate Factory,* and there's this cooking project we started yesterday, and there are those thank-you letters to write, and Mrs. So-'n-so is coming in to practice the play—how are we ever going to fit all this in?"—knowing that we won't.

D Whenever I've been in your classroom, most of the children seem to be doing things they identify with pretty strongly.

J I would say that three-quarters of our day is spent doing things we personally identify with. Last spring, for example, baseball was on many of the boys' minds. I think I may have reinforced this by going to a Red Sox game myself and then bringing in all kinds of materials for a baseball collage. I also read to them some baseball books that a child from a previous class had written, and the children were very excited by these books, so I got a spate of illustrated baseball books. Baseball is often a family interest, of course, and the boys, especially, get lots of encouragement from their fathers. Children often get hooked on these various personal interest themes, which can occupy them for quite a few days.

> *I would say that three-quarters of our day is spent doing things we personally identify with*

D I know that some themes infect the entire class and can go on for quite long periods.

J I think a good example would be all the activity generated by the Camelot play. We were involved with that for about six weeks. It began with one of the parents from last year's class who often visited our room and especially enjoyed listening to us sing one of our favorite songs, "Morning Has Broken." This year she was working at the high school with one of the English teachers. It so happened that the English class was studying myths and legends, including the story of the Garden of Eden. The parent suggested to the teacher that my class might like to come to the high school and sing "Morning Has Broken," which deals with the Garden of Eden story. We had a great time, and the result was that the English teacher invited us to put on a play for her class, maybe something to do with King Arthur and the Round Table, because they were going to be studying the Arthurian legend. The idea got around, and soon a mother, who was involved in drama in the community, had volunteered to help the children develop the play. So the Camelot project didn't come from the children. It came from me, and from the mothers, and the high school teacher. Already the high school teacher and I are making plans for a different joint activity for next year, and that project will come partly from me too, but it will be based on what I know children naturally seem to enjoy. Of course, I don't know how it will work out, and there will probably be lots of changes.

> *if the idea appeals to them, they'll take it over, shape it, and make it their own*

R  It seems to me that your decision to do a Camelot play for a high school class or to do some other literature project next year is not very different from a decision to put clay or sand or paints in your classroom. From research and from experience we know that young children generally respond to these activities. We can never quite predict what they will do with them, but we do know that if an idea or an activity appeals to them, they'll take it over, shape it, and make it their own.

J  I know that I always have my eye open for things that might interest the children. Shortly before Christmas last year I happened to stop in at my poet friend Sam Cornish's bookstore and saw this miniature paper book, about 2" x 2". It had just two or three stitches holding it together and a tiny design on the cover. It was just darling, but it wasn't for children—it was for adults. I bought it and took it to school and showed it to the children, and they loved it, maybe because it was so small. We talked about why the cover design was appropriate for that size book and why a larger design wouldn't work because part of it would be cut off. Pretty soon lots of miniature books with miniature designs on them began to appear, and soon we decided that miniature books would be good stocking stuffers for our parents. Many of the children made little books for that purpose and wrote stories to go in them—mostly holiday stories—and I rewrote the stories in the books in standard form, putting the original texts at the back, and the children did the miniature drawings inside. They were just precious. Now that activity just happened to come up. I didn't say, "All right, now we're going to learn about miniature books, so we can all go and make one." It was so much better than this business of having to dream up some holiday gift for the children to make for their parents.

**D** If you had asked the children to come up with gift ideas for their parents, they would probably have thought of something they already knew how to make. The miniature book idea involved them in investigating a new concept—the concept of scale—without their being taught that concept.

**J** I really wasn't thinking about scale, so I guess you could say we got into it indirectly. The children get into lots of things indirectly. I generally use some of Gerald McDermott's books which show artwork and design from various cultures, African, Japanese, etc. He does beautiful page designs, and I show these to the children and we talk about them—what the designer did to make the page attractive, the colors he used, and the shapes, how he arranged them on the page, what writing he used and where he put it. Pretty soon I begin to notice some of these things appearing in the children's work. They begin to do designs that are similar, experimenting with things they have seen and talked about. Now these things don't come from lessons. I don't decide, all right, now we're going to study design or now we're going to do Picasso. I guess I have in the

back of my mind the idea that sometime we're going to talk about design, and we do it when something comes up that makes it seem natural and appropriate.

[D] You've mentioned several themes that have involved the children for varying lengths of time. I know there are many activities that you haven't mentioned.

[J] A lot of our time is spent in drama, painting, math, cooking, singing, moving to music, building with blocks, constructing with various materials, and then of course there's the writing, and I think that happens because so many other things are happening.

[D] The writing blends with those various expressive activities because it's basically expressive. It's very different from the writing children do in response to an assignment—like reporting on a book, or a science investigation, or a summer holiday, or a trip to the fire station.

[J] Children need opportunity for spontaneous expression in writing, and it needs to be free to flow into and out of other expressive activities. When my children get going with their writing, I hate to interrupt them, so I generally don't. Instead, I think about ways to carry it forward. In this connection felt pens have been tremendously important. I used to think I didn't need them, that crayons would do just as well, but there's something about those pens—thin ones and thick ones, in as many colors as I can find—there's a sense in which the children seem to paint with them. There's all that color and brightness and flow, and the colors go on fast and easily and without the mess of paints, and of course they dry fast and don't need to be hung up the way paintings do. And the children work together more easily around their felt pen drawings, whereas only one child (two at most) would stand at the easel to paint. And they talk

*there's all that color and brightness and flow*

together about their drawings, because there's usually more to talk about than with a painting, and then the writing flows out of the talking and drawing. Sometimes the writing gets sloppy, and the children cross out and make blots, but I've learned to expect that and accept it. For a time I tried to get them to write in pencil so that they could erase and their papers wouldn't get to look so bad, but they much prefer the felt pens. They love to use them in illustrating books. They even decorate the text as well as illustrating it. I know those pens enhance the flow of reading, writing, and drawing.

[D] That word "flow" intrigues me—a flow involving talking, drawing, and writing.

[R] If we reflect on the fact that words come out of people either through their mouths or through their fingers, what strikes me about your children is that mouths and fingers are close together. Your children move from talking to drawing to writing to talking to writing to drawing. Each seems to be a natural extension of the other. The words and pictures come tripping out of their felt pens almost as easily as they come tripping out of their mouths, perhaps with a little more struggle because they're learning to talk in a new medium. Maybe that's why they don't have to struggle with what to write about; they're excited about these different ways of saying what's on their minds.

> *they're learning to talk in a new medium*

[J] I believe that children, unlike many adults, have a real need to think aloud. I've always tried to help children understand that their own speech can be written down—that that's what writing is—but more recently I began to appreciate how important it is to let children draw a lot and talk with each other while they draw. I mean all children, and especially nonreaders or those who are having trouble learning to read. I know that I must let them draw, let them express. I know that if I do this, these children will eventually read. I still feel that I don't fully understand this, but I can see it in my children, this flow of ideas, this coming out, through speech and through the hand and onto paper. First the thoughts come out in one form, and then they come out in another, mixed together. And this seems to be just as true of those who learn to read easily as of those who have more struggle. I sometimes think of what I've read about the brain—that the left side is supposed to be for language and the right side for feeling, action, and perception. If that's so, my children's brains must be flip-flopping at a great rate. The children we really need to worry about are those that don't express themselves in any way.

> *their brains must be flip-flopping at a great rate*

[D] I'm wondering about the significance of the *amount* of such expression, and the quality, as an indication of a child's readiness for reading.

[J] I think there's a general connection, that for most children writing and drawing seem to be a natural pathway into reading, but generalizing about other things, such as how much they write, or how creative they are, or how neat they are, can be pretty risky; there are so many individual variations. For me the important point is that when various expressive opportunities are available, each child will do what he feels ready and able to do, and there's no pressure to express in one mode more than another. What I'm finding is that when children are free in this way, they all eventually begin to write, and the writing leads quite naturally into reading.

[D] The absence of pressure strikes me as being a vital part of all this.

[J] Occasionally, as a little experiment, I ask the children whether they'd prefer to work on their reading or work on their writing and drawing. They almost always choose the writing and drawing. There's less pressure there. They don't have to be so exact, they can't be wrong. If they're reading and they come to a word they don't know, they have to stop; they might get stuck; they might make a mistake. But not so with the writing and drawing and talking. There they're free to move from one mode to another, and if they're not ready to write, they don't have to. I notice that the more expressive activities seem especially attractive to children first thing in the morning. The more passive activities, such as listening and reading, are not nearly so popular at that time of day. I remember one group of boys in particular last year. The first thing they did in the morning was get together and draw. The drawing seemed to be something that enabled them to talk to one another. It was a very social thing. There they were, gathered around a table or sprawled on the floor, drawing and talking, partly about what they were drawing and partly about other things. All I know is that it seemed very gripping to them, and if I interrupted, as I sometimes had to, maybe to record attendance, they groaned.

R  Yet they were constantly interrupting each other with their own talking. Maybe these were the natural interruptions that helped to carry their work along, but they resented what they saw as the unnatural interruptions that stopped them short and broke their trains of thought.

J  That's why I hate all the unnatural interruptions in the school day—like children being taken out for this "special" program or that: remedial reading, speech, English as a second language, and so on. Even the programs they really enjoy, such as gym and art and music, are at times seen by the children as interruptions of important activity. It must be puzzling to them to be told to stop drawing because it's time to go to art! As for the non-English-speaking children, they get taken out of a climate where everyone is speaking the language to spend half an hour with other non-English-speaking children in order to learn the language! And everyone knows that young children

*that's why I hate all the unnatural interruptions in the school day*

best learn a language by being in an environment where everyone is speaking it. I must add, however, that many of the specialists are helpful, but I wish that they could work in the classroom with the children. That way I could learn something from them.

[D] Much of your children's expressive work originates in their own heads, in their own personal experiences, often outside of school. Some of their writing and drawing is very personal.

[J] That's true, but if you look beneath these personal differences, you often can find some common themes, and I'm noticing how certain themes seem to recur from year to year, especially around holiday times. At Halloween, for example, we get the ghosts, the masks, the sharks, the skeletons, the scary things taking over the world. There's danger, darkness, death, fear of the unknown, fear of things bigger than themselves, concern about whether something is real or unreal. Some of this is gay and happy, but a lot of it is grim and gruesome. We get some of these concerns again at Christmas, with the various catastrophes that happen to Santa Claus, and we get some at St. Patrick's Day, with the leprechauns. The holidays seem to highlight these issues, and many of the children's deep concerns come out indirectly through holiday stories. The children don't need to say, "I'm afraid of this or that"; they write about somebody else or some thing that is afraid. And there's this theme of power, which appeared in so many of the Camelot books: "I'm so small and adults are so big, and they're always telling me what to do." But when the children act out Sir Lancelot and Superman, or draw and write about them, the children take charge in ways that are safe. They know they're not ready to take charge in real life.

*they know they're not ready to take charge in real life*

[R] There are children who have special difficulties, real problems to cope with, which seem to come out in their writing. I think immediately of Billy facing the death of his father.

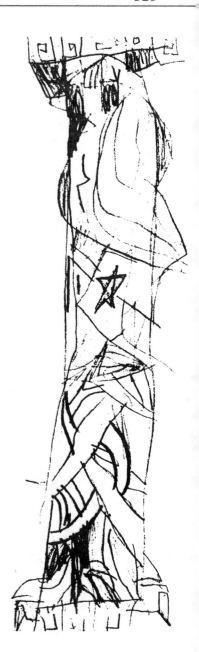

Billy is certainly an example I'll never forget. His mother felt, as I did, that he was able to deal with this problem—was able to get a lot of those feelings out through his stories, his drawings, and his writing. A lot more came out that way than through anything he said, either at home or at school. Very little of this would have been possible in a basal reader approach to reading, or even in a language experience approach. Every single book that he wrote revealed, in some way, his concern about what was happening at home. In November he wrote My Thanksgiving Book. The Thanksgiving meal was the last time that his father was able to come to the table, and I think that his mother must have talked with him about how Thanksgiving is a time when we give thanks for the good things we have, and Billy worked this idea into his book. When he finished it he asked me how I liked it, and I wrote that I liked it very much. Then he showed it to Barbara (my aide), and she wrote that she liked it very much. Then he showed it to his grandmother and to his mother, and they both wrote something in it. Then he showed it to his father, and his father wrote something in it, something very personal. This was probably the last written communication that Billy had from his father. Between Thanksgiving and Christmas he wrote Santa Is Sick, in which Santa gets sick but still "makes it." I guess Billy was then hoping that his father might still make it. But his father died, shortly before Christmas.

During the next several months Billy wrote a number of other books in which various troubles appeared; for example, his book about the Flintstones getting robbed and his book about Mr. and Mrs. Frankenstein's adventures while working in a cemetery. When we first learned that Billy's father was not going to live—Billy talked about this at school—I decided to read *Annie and the Old One* to the children. It's a marvelous story about a Navaho Indian girl whose grandmother is dying. Her mother is weaving a blanket. The grandmother tells the little girl that when the blanket is finished, she (the grandmother) will go to Mother Earth. So the child tries to prevent the finishing of the blanket. It's a beautiful story. I've used it in working with teachers, many of whom have said, "Oh, I'd never use that with children," but over the years I've used it a number of times. Several weeks later I brought the story out again, and some of the children said, "Oh, we've heard that one before," but Billy said, "Read it again, it's my favorite story." And as I read, he continually interrupted to tell us what was going to happen. He remembered every detail, almost verbatim, particularly the part about the death and going to Mother Earth. When we finished it he said, "Can I take that home for the weekend?" and I said yes, because I knew that his parents were very supportive of what we were doing. He wanted to take the book to Mr. Blaney (the principal), which he did, and Mr. Blaney went through the book with him while Billy told him the whole story.

About that same time Billy's father called the family together and said, "I have so much pain that I don't want to live; I'm ready to die," and Billy was in on this. He told us about it at school, and Mr. Blaney talked with him about the fact that his father was in so much pain. I did too, and I think that Billy came to accept the idea that it was better for his father to be free of all that pain. It was about that time that he wrote The Pain Book. His final book, which to me is the most touching, was called The Disaster Book. He wrote it late in the spring, when his family was getting ready to move to another country, and in this book Billy recounted one disaster after another, each one related to something actually happening in his personal life. In earlier books he was coping through fantasy, but in this book he described what was actually happening to him. On the last page he wrote, "And the worst thing is when they all happen at once."

*on the last page he wrote, "And the worst thing is when they all happen at once"*

[D] I find that account very moving, partly because I knew Billy from my several visits to your class that year. I think it must take a great deal of experience to be able to handle a situation like that with such sensitivity.

[J] I did keep in close touch with Billy's mother, which I think was essential. Our way of helping him at school was partly an extension of the open manner in which the family was coping. I'm not certain about how I would manage in circumstances in which home and school philosophies were far apart.

[R] I will never forget working in your classroom that particular year. I know that you went through a great deal of personal anguish as you wrestled with the problem of how best to help Billy. I also know that some teachers would have chosen a very different approach. But something about what you did reminds me of what I'd like to talk about next. It seems to me that you invested in Billy's strength as a human being, his strength to live through personal tragedy and come out of it a stronger child. I think that you regularly invest in children's strengths, all kinds of strengths, but particularly the strength of their ideas. Your curriculum—the things the children think about and do—comes from inside their heads, and yours. This is basically very different from what happens in most classrooms where the curriculum comes from outside the children—from textbooks, from workbooks, from the school system syllabus, from various learning materials that lead the child, and often the teacher as well, down some predetermined path.

> *you regularly invest in children's strengths . . . particularly the strength of their ideas*

[D] I find the word "invest"' quite helpful—that teachers invest in certain practices they believe in, that they think will work, that will achieve certain results. You could say that traditionally most teachers have invested in written-down

curriculums, in oral recitations, in written tests. Many schools and teachers currently are investing in curriculum kits of one kind or another. Ten years ago we were struggling to help teachers free children from the dictates of rigid curriculum. And the teacher could get out of the role of orchestra leader, we saw, and into the role of adviser and facilitator.

R In those days we were helping teachers invest in children's pursuit of their own learning, invest in choice, invest in various raw materials through which children might carry on direct investigations of the physical world. These were vital beginnings. I think Jeanette is now discovering more about how she can invest in children's ideas and how these ideas, together with her own, can become the ongoing curriculum.

J I'm finding big changes in my ideas about how time should be spent. Now that I'm not planning to do math every day, or any other subject every day, I've come to see that it's really a lot better to have a long math session two or three times a week, because once the children get involved in math, just as in reading or writing, they love it and want to stay with it. It's my decision that we have math—but I talk with the children about whether they'd like a short math period every day or a longer period less often, and they prefer the longer period.

I also recognize that I'm much more holistic in my approach now than I used to be. I have a picture in my mind of how one thing melts into another. I used to go along with the idea that in a learner-centered classroom there should be a math area, a science area, an art area, a language area, etc.; that a child would choose one of these areas and work in it for a while, and when he tired of it or finished what he was doing, would go to another area; and that he would be expected to think about what he was going to do in each area, make plans, be responsible for following through with a chosen activity. I now see that process as somewhat artificial, not in keeping with the way a child's mind works. A child doesn't think to himself, "Now I'm going to do a math activity, and then I'll do a science activity." He doesn't sort life out that way, although adults may expect him to behave as though he does. The child naturally does what makes sense to him at the moment, and his focus is much more specific. There's a way in which those traditional subject-matter categories can fragment a child's attention, particularly when they're seen as a basis for carving up the classroom space and for labeling materials and activities.

In the past we talked a lot about "extensions"—the importance of a teacher's being able to extend whatever a child might get into, say with blocks or sand or water. I now think the teacher doesn't need to extend an activity; the children extend it. The teacher's extension ideas are often interrupting. If I ask a child a question about something she's built with blocks, she will answer my question, or if I suggest something that she might do with the blocks, she may do what I suggest, but as soon as she's done it, she'll go right back to what she was doing in the first place. I think we're fooling ourselves by trying to extend some of these things. The child's ideas are real for her; our ideas often seem fakey.

> *the child's ideas are real to her; our ideas often seem fakey*

$\boxed{R}$ The fakeyness may come from our ulterior motives. If a child has built a magnificent block tower, and you ask him to count the blocks (because you feel you'd better sneak some math into his project), you can't expect him to be wildly enthusiastic about your suggestion. But if you appreciate his tower for what it is and for what it represents to him, you've got the basis for nonfakey communication, and then everybody's ideas get a better hearing. When your children are given time for these activities, they're not doing them to learn skills. They're doing them for their own sake. The skills get learned,

> *the skills get learned, but the learning is incidental to the activity*

but the learning is incidental to the activity. And that's very different from an approach in which all the children are expected to focus on a certain skill at a certain time and to follow a predetermined path in learning the set of skills. Or each child is assessed, "diagnosed," and placed in a particular place in the prescribed sequence.

|J| The words "diagnosing" and "prescribing" don't fit what I do and why I do it. For one thing, they're medical terms, and the doctor is usually focusing on what's wrong. A diagnosis is generally done on someone who's sick.

"You've got an earache? Better take penicillin."

"Don't know your short vowels? Here, do this exercise."

|R| The investments are very different. In a "diagnostic prescriptive" approach the teacher invests in knowing that when a child has gone through one step she can prescribe the next—it's there in the book and the steps are generally what some "expert" thinks the steps ought to be. They're the connections he sees in what he's trying to get the children to learn. When *you* invest in children's ideas, you're not sure what the next step is going to be, because you're not sure what connections the children are going to make—and it's the connections in their heads that count when they learn something.

> *the steps are generally what some "expert" thinks, logically, they ought to be*

|J| I do try to sense these connections when I'm trying to help a child learn something that he seems ready for. At times I give pretty specific and positive direction to some children. I know that sometimes a child needs to be nudged in order to begin doing what he's capable of doing. This might sound prescriptive, but it seems to me that in an environment where one hears the occasional prescription, "Johnny, try this, do that," it is very different from an environment in which prescriptions are the general rule.

D Many people take comfort in knowing that a child's learning is being carefully programmed at school. They assume that if steps A, B, and C are important, and a child does those steps and gets the right answers, he's learning. But right answers are such flimsy, inadequate evidence of the quality of a child's learning. The visible symptoms can be so misleading.

J In any kind of classroom, it's always easier to say what children are *doing* than to say what they're learning. Maybe I don't know what a child is learning at any particular time or what she is ready for at that moment, but as I get to know children as individuals I get a sense of what they're *learning,* what they're ready for, what I can expect. I know from experience that children are interested in the natural world and that they enjoy making things from natural materials. I know they're interested in art and music, sports, and space, and in things that happened long ago and far away—like dinosaurs—and in the way other cultures do things, and even in my life as a child as well as in my life as an adult. And increasingly I discover that they know things I'm ignorant of. To sum it up, we do things together that we care about, and the specific learnings come along, mostly as by-products of the activity.

> *it's always easier to say what children are doing than to say what they're learning*

D Suppose that you were to scale your educational priorities, arrange them in order of importance, as a practical guideline to the decisions that you make each day in the classroom. What would you put at the top of the list?

J If you're looking for a practical guideline, then I guess I'd say that I want my children to take responsibility for their own learning, which means they must feel in charge of themselves, know that they can take initiative. The critical thing is that the children know that their ideas matter to me.

> *the critical thing is that the children know that their ideas matter to me*

*R* But don't *your* ideas matter too, right along with the children's? When you walked into Sam's bookstore and saw that miniature book and picked it off the shelf, you saw that book as an idea to be shared with your children. Because you are investing in children's ideas, perhaps you are freed up to invest in your own. I don't think that teachers who invest in somebody else's curriculum feel free to do that, because the curriculum is so overpowering. What I see happening in your classroom is that you're continually risking your own ideas. Sometimes they blend in, and sometimes they don't, in which case you're quite prepared to drop them.

*D* So we're talking about an organic curriculum, one that unfolds with the life of the group, not a curriculum imposed from outside. I think it would be useful if we could pull together our reasons for believing in the organic approach. Rosemary just mentioned one reason, having to do with the gradual buildup of connections in a child's head. At the beginning of this discussion Jeanette mentioned another when she said that she wants the children to have a full and happy life in a classroom where all kinds of learning can take place. I wonder if you would say a bit more about that, Jeanette, about your reasons for wanting that full life and that broad-based learning. I know there's more in it than your personal preference and taste.

*J* I think that children learn best when they're deeply involved, and they don't get deeply involved unless they strongly identify with what they're doing. They don't identify with somebody else's projects the way they do with their own. So it's this depth of involvement that I strive for.

*D* How about broader social goals? When you say that you want the children to feel in charge of themselves and to take responsibility for their own learning, I know that you are talking about more than just learning to read.

*J* Yes, of course. I am thinking about their development as people and as citizens. I think our society would be stronger and healthier if children grew up feeling in charge of themselves, feeling free and responsible, not just for their learning but for all kinds of behavior.

*D* I know that not everyone agrees with that. There are many people who think that children are irresponsible almost by nature, and such people are quite happy to have children earn their freedom through years of dutiful obedience and direction-following in school. And there are others who believe in a society of leaders and drones and are quite content to have a school system that helps to produce it. The 3R curriculum, after all, took root in a society that needed a literate workforce for the nation's factories, and the 3R curriculum is still what drives the machine.

*J* Well, those are not my ideas of what children are like, and that's certainly not my vision of what our society ought to be, or needs to be, or can afford to be. I guess I try to encourage all the children to feel like leaders, and by that I mean that I want them all to know that they make unique contributions to the life of the classroom. I try to treat them with the same respect that I think we should all show toward each other. To me it seems obvious that this way of working is best for children right now and best for all of us in the future.

Still, as you point out, not everyone agrees with my educational values and goals, and from time to time I get uptight about this. I don't get anxious about the basic rightness of what I'm doing—I have no doubts about that—but about the jarring that occurs with the system. I have the children for just one year, and that's not enough. Soon they encounter the conflicting philosophy of traditional school. I fret about that and sometimes get angry about it. We have all this schoolwide testing, and

> *our society would be stronger and healthier if children grew up feeling in charge of themselves*

> *I try to treat them with the same respect that I think we should all show toward each other*

I get worried about the children going on to another teacher who will be expecting that they know certain things, and there's this big concern about "Who is not ready for second grade?" and "Who ought to repeat first grade?" and I hate all of that. The parents begin getting anxious and start wondering what teacher their child will have next year, and some of them wonder whether their child will be behind because he's had this kind of program with me. I get very tense about it. Every year it's the same way. One day I get all tense about all those workbooks my children haven't had, so I get them out of the closet and give them out. A few of the children zip straight through them, and some stay with them for about a day and then lose interest, and then, somehow, I get over my anxiety and we're back to normal.

|D| You mean that everything really turns out all right, that you needn't have been anxious?

|J| No, I'm not saying that. I guess I'm saying that I learn to live with my anxieties, because there are certain things I just can't compromise about. I don't believe in all this testing and judging and sorting children out, and I don't believe in holding a child back just because he hasn't learned certain skills in reading or math or handwriting. I don't believe that my job is to get children ready for second grade. That's much too narrow, too limiting. But not everybody sees it that way, so I go on being anxious. But above my anxieties I carry a certain faith, based on experience, that if children are genuinely turned on to things that interest them, they will learn far more than if I program them, judge them, and test them, but it will be a much broader kind of learning, not just the skill things that so many teachers hammer on.

> *above my anxieties I carry a certain faith*

# MATHEMATICAL INTERLUDE

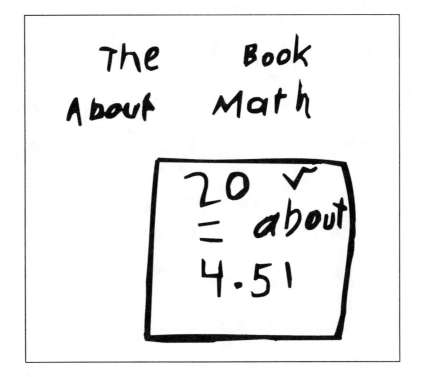

*Three pages from Nicky's book*

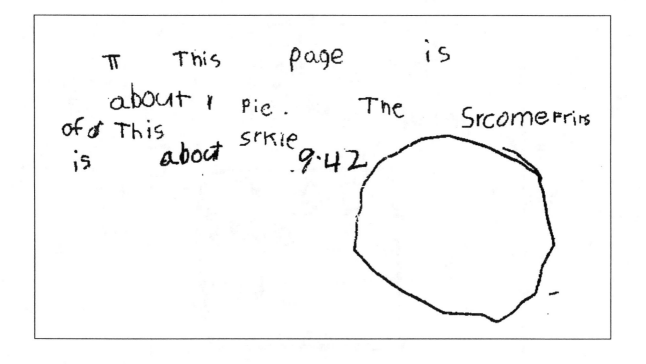

π This page is about π pie. The srcomerris of This is about srkie .9.42

This page is about dvididby. ÷

$27 \div 8 = 3$ and a remobo of 3.

$87 \div 17 = 5$ and a remad of 2.

$105 \div 7 = 15$ and a remada of 0.

is my About
rc my #oby the is Author
That why I math
Book I was rot This
This Book hoping That
Published ?? Wold get

# DISCUSSION 2

*– we talk about things social and emotional –*

Every classroom is in some sense a community and has, for better or worse, some kind of community spirit. This spirit is what makes one class operate differently from another, even though the classrooms may look alike, be identically provisioned, follow the same curriculum, and even when the teachers use similar words (such as "developmentally appropriate") to describe their philosophies. I have in mind a spirit that is deeply imbedded in the way people feel about each other, talk with each other, act toward each other. It is implicit in everything that happens. This community spirit, and things contributing to it, will be seen as the unifying theme of our second discussion as Jeanette continues to talk about her classroom.

## Serious Purpose, Natural Honesty, and Joy

[D] In our last discussion you told us a lot about what the children do. They're always doing so much that I've never stopped to think about what they might not be allowed to do. I suppose you have some rules, but I'm not quite sure what they are.

[J] I guess I do have rules: I don't allow the children to run around the room or punch and poke one another. And I don't like them feeling one another's heads, because lice go round from time to time. I talk to them a lot about using inside voices, so that we don't disturb classes down the hall. I don't like them to make noise in the hallways when we're going past other teachers' rooms; I don't want them to eat their snacks after eleven o'clock, because it's too close to lunch time (before that they can snack whenever they wish). They're not allowed to spit. They're not allowed to call one another names; this is one thing they will report one another about, partly, I suppose, because Mr. Blaney makes a big thing of it. I don't like them to tease in a way that hurts another child's feelings, and I think I'm rather moralistic about saying thank you. I don't want a great chanting of thank yous, but I do like individual children to say thank you when they receive something. I encourage children to settle their differences peacefully, not just to apologize by saying I'm sorry, but to take time to talk things out. When we're in a group I'm very particular that they don't talk when other children are talking. I must really drive this one home, because in the Camelot play, when the children were suggesting laws to be brought to the Round Table, someone suggested "Jimmy Carter's law"—Don't Hurt Poor People—and someone else proposed "Mrs. Amidon's law"—Don't Interrupt. I make quite a thing about cleaning up and not leaving big messes for Mr. Quigley (the

> *they're not allowed to spit or to call one another names or to leave big messes for Mr. Quigley*

custodian). I'm also particular about not wasting materials. I get really cross if the children are careless with the felt pens and with paper—I'm always talking with them about trees being cut down. Some of the children come from homes where they have lots of things, and I think they need to be more aware of waste.

**D** I notice that most of these rules have to do with social behavior.

**J** Well, when I think about work, I'd rather call them expectations. I have the expectation, for example, that children will read every day, alone or with someone else, and that they will take part in the math sessions that we have several times a week. When they begin to show interest in certain materials, with the spelling materials, for example, I begin to have expectations about their use, not for all children but for those who are ready. Occasionally I might give them something specific, like a handwriting paper, and expect them to get it finished sometime during the morning. Sometimes a child won't get it done, so he'll have to finish it in the afternoon or next morning. I sometimes think this happens because children have so little sense of time. The day just slips away, and they have so much on their minds. Unless I say, "We're all going to do the handwriting paper right now," I feel that I can't hold them to it, because of this lack of a sense of time. When we sing they're all expected to come up and sing, and the same when we read a story—although there's never any problem there, because they all love to sing and to listen to stories. In general, when something begins to go well, I have expectations that it will continue to go well, and I get caught up with the enthusiasm of the activity.

> *I have an expectation that children will read every day*

**D** How about an example of an enthusiasm you get caught up with?

|J| I love to read to children, and I think I know a lot about children's literature. So I expect that children will respond to what I read, and from experience I know the kinds of things they enjoy. We read lots of poetry, chosen from various anthologies. And lots of short stories, usually related to the various festivals and holidays as they come along or to some theme or interest that happens to come up. I also read longer books, such as *Stuart Little* and *Charlotte's Web*. Year after year the children's all-time favorite author is Roald Dahl. They love *James and the Giant Peach,* also *Charlie and the Chocolate Factory, Charlie and the Great Glass Elevator, Danny, the Champion of the World,* and *The Fantastic Mr. Fox.* I'm sure that part of the appeal is that these longer books come in chapters. So we read a little bit, and then it's time for recess or time to go home and we have to stop, and then we come back to it, like a radio or TV serial, and the children get caught up in the story, and I do too.

|R| When you say that you get caught up in the story, I think you're talking about something very important. The children sense your enjoyment, which is part of their getting to know you as a person.

|J| I think they should know me as a person. I'm much more natural in my relationship with the children now than I used to be, and more honest in my responses. Lots of personal things get talked about during the course of the day. Like yesterday, I happened to mention that the two of you were coming for dinner tonight, and I told them that another teacher they knew was coming too. They were really interested. And they're interested in my clothes—someone always comments when I have on anything that's new or different—and they know I like to grow things and have flowers around. They know I have a sense of humor; not a day goes by without our having a good laugh. I used to duck questions about my age, but I don't

> *the children get caught up in the story, and I do too*

> *I'm more natural in my relationship with the children now . . . and more honest in my responses*

anymore. The other day two of the Jewish girls asked me about my religious beliefs and whether I go to church. I sensed that they wanted more than a yes or no answer, so I told them that when I was a little girl I went to a Christian church with my mother and father, and that later on I went to a church where there were Christian and Jewish people, and that right now I'm not going to church, but I still have some very strong beliefs. They seemed satisfied with that answer.

**D** Being honest and natural with children makes so much sense to me as a basic attitude for adults to have, but how honest should you be when you're dealing with sensitive topics, with a child's questions about sex, for example, or divorce?

**J** I try to keep in mind the age and developmental levels of the children and what they're able to handle. I used to think that children might be damaged by frank discussion, but through experience I have come to see that a child takes from a discussion what he is ready to take, especially if the adult doesn't go into things the child isn't asking about. If a child asks a question about sex, I don't launch into a long discourse. I answer simply and proceed slowly, feeling my way, trying to get a sense of what the child is really asking. I try to read the child's body language, the way he looks and responds. Generally I can sense what the child is really asking and how much he really wants to know.

**D** Can you think of other examples of how you're more natural in your relationship with the children now than you used to be?

**J** Yes, the way I greet them in the morning. The usual procedure at the school where I am now is for all the children to wait outside until the bell rings, then file in 15 minutes before classes begin. I have always wanted my children to be free to come into the room as soon as they arrive at school, if they want to, and when I asked Mr. Blaney if this could happen, he was immediately agreeable, providing I am in the room when the first child arrives. My old approach would have been to stand at the classroom door each morning and greet the children as they arrived, and I would have talked to them and asked them what they had done the previous evening and what they thought they might get into today. That was my main reason for having them come in early—to help them focus on plans for the day—and that probably was in my mind when I first talked with Mr. Blaney. But the whole procedure has become much more natural. I'm in the room working, and a child comes through the door. I don't stop and turn my whole attention to her, as I used to, and the child may or may not come over to talk to me. I don't think I could stand by the door now and say good morning to each child and expect the child to say "Good morning, Mrs. Amidon," and then ask the kinds of questions I don't really care about anyway, like "What did you have for breakfast today?" Years ago I often felt that I was dragging comments from them. I now see the artificiality of my questions. They know I'm there, and they know I'm available to them if they need me, but they don't feel under observation or about to be questioned. Besides, they know I'm getting ready for my day.

$\boxed{R}$ When you put it like that, it does underline how differently we treat children from the way we treat each other. Imagine being asked each morning what you've had for breakfast!

$\boxed{J}$ Another example of ways in which I think I'm more natural with children now is that I don't have fakey discussions with them anymore—well, maybe I still do, but not often—pointing out morals, for example, or the "Now I'm going to help you understand it" type of discussion. And when I do those things now, I find myself saying to the children, "Gosh, don't I

> *I don't have fakey discussions with them anymore*

sound just like a schoolteacher!" I think I'm much more aware now of what I'm doing.

[D] Say a little more about the difference between fakey and nonfakey in that context.

[J] I think some of my fakier discussions may have come from books, from stories with morals or lessons, where I would make sure that the moral got pointed out. I don't plan these little lessons anymore. Now, when I'm reading to the children, it's much more likely that a child says something—probably something I hadn't thought about—and this triggers a response in me that leads to a short discussion which is spontaneous and natural. The children sense my naturalness, so they tend to say what they really think instead of what teacher would like to hear. Those little interruptions can be very important for the children's development, because they occur naturally and are triggered by something that has caught a child's attention.

[R] There's a way in which "those little interruptions," as you call them, are continually happening in your room, not just when you're reading to them, but in all sorts of social situations. The children are continually having to make social and moral decisions of one kind or another.

*the children are continually having to make social and moral decisions*

[J] That's true, and it's also true that we're not role-playing in order to learn how to live together. The situations are real, so their decisions are real. I think the children feel responsibility and take it seriously. If anyone has a spill or breaks something accidentally, there's a run of people to help. That's very different from "Oh Mrs. Amidon, Kim spilled the paint!" This is a change in my classroom in the last three years. I don't mean that they never tattle about things, which I suppose is all part of how children develop conscience, but when something serious does happen, their impulse now is to run to help rather than to run to tell. And last year there was that stealing episode. When I confronted Larry, he immediately said, "Yes, I did it." My past experience has been denial, denial, denial, unless I've had the evidence right there. But as soon as I said something to Larry, he said "Yes, I did it, and it's not the only time I did it." He knew that I strongly disapproved of his action and was very upset by it and was disappointed, but he didn't feel unloved or rejected. There was a trust there that had been built up, because the children know that they are accepted, by me and by their friends. So Larry knew that I would try to help him not do it again.

---

*acceptance is coupled with positive expectations*

---

[R] Perhaps he also knew that you expected him to want to behave differently and to be able to behave differently. When acceptance is coupled with positive expectations, children are helped (like the rest of us) to feel their own strength—even to find strength they didn't know they had.

[J] I think that acceptance helps children feel safe, safe with adults, safe with each other. In my class last year I had a little girl, Martha, whose writing was outstanding. Her mother came in and told me that on the previous evening Martha had said, "I really think that Ellen writes the best stories in our class, Mother." And her mother added, "I really think she believes that. I don't think she considers herself to be superior in that way at all, and I'm so glad that she doesn't." I had another child who couldn't read a word, and I don't think he considered himself to be inferior, and I doubt that even Martha was aware that he couldn't read—well, in a way she realized it, but she didn't see herself as superior to him. She couldn't put him down because he was in the low reading group, because we don't have reading groups. I really think he was quite philosophical about not being able to read. It's not that I'm trying to shield children from their strengths and weaknesses. It's that I don't point them up.

R Perhaps the child who felt philosophical about not being able to read could feel that way because he felt confidence in his ability to learn. You'd given him no reason to doubt that he could learn to read and every reason to expect that he eventually would.

J A very different thing having to do with acceptance is the children's willingness to take on roles of the opposite sex in their drama. This is new for me. I think of two girls, very feminine girls, who took on the role of page boys, and of Jeff, who took on the role of Mother Pig. The children felt safe to experiment this way, without fear of being laughed at by their friends.

D There was a similar development in my last fifth grade class. Along about January Barbara asked if she might bring in one of her favorite records, and Peter said he'd be willing to bring in his record player. The next day the record was played at recess, and several children, including Barbara and Peter, stayed inside to listen. That was the beginning. On the second or third day two of the children began dancing to the music. Soon others were joining in, and within a week no one wanted to go outside for recess; everyone wanted to stay inside and dance or watch the dancing. A week or so later the dancing expanded into dance drama, which began with what Peter called "Cinderella at the Rock Concert." (I had recently read Perrault's original *Cinderella* to the children, which inspired two of the boys to write their own modernized versions.) Each day the Cinderella drama unfolded in different ways as the children traded parts and experimented with different versions of the characters and plot. They took this all very seriously, while having loads of fun. After about a month the Cinderella theme gave way to a restaurant theme, which lasted, on and off, for the rest of the school year. Throughout all of this I was an interested and supportive bystander, who occasionally joined in the

> *I tried to give the children space to do the things they wanted to do*

dancing. I would like to think that the atmosphere of that classroom, as it developed during the year, was not unlike the atmosphere in your room, Jeanette. Certainly the children weren't being programmed through a lot of academic stuff, and lots of projects just seemed to unfold, and there was a similar flow of expressive activity. I tried to give the children space to do things they wanted to do.

[R] I'm sure you're referring to more than just physical space, but even physical space—the lack of it—can have a negative effect on children's behavior in school. If you think about this room that the three of us are sitting in now, it's about the size of many classrooms. Imagine that there were twenty of us confined here every day except Saturday and Sunday—

[J] And confined to desks!

[R] Some of the day being able to do things we like to do and some of the day having to do things we hate to do. Soon we'd all have cabin fever, and within a short time some of us would probably be sick. Yet we expect children to be able to take such confinement. When you remarked earlier that one of your objectives is to help the children have a happy life, I was thinking how difficult that is to achieve within the four walls of a classroom.

[J] I do let the children move freely around the room and go into the hallway to get a drink when they want to and go to the john when they want to, and we're lucky to have an outside door so that in good weather the activities can spill outside. I know that the children need privacy too. One of their favorite spots is that small space between the piano and the mailboxes. From there the children can see out into the hall and across the hall onto the playground, but they're separated from the rest of the classroom. It isn't that they're doing anything there they shouldn't be doing. They may choose to go there and read or do math or just be alone for a while.

R  I read an article recently that described some research suggesting a direct link between physical confinement and violence. The research samples seemed to indicate that people who are violent as adults tend to be those who experienced insufficient physical movement when they were infants—like the children who are picked up just to be fed, then put down again and left; the children who are static for long periods of their infancy, without the normal kinds of stimulation. I can imagine those same children going into first grade and being made to sit all day long at their desks, not moving, not talking, doing what they're told.

D  This idea of space—for me it's powerful. Not just physical space to move around in, but time space—the time to move and the freedom to move. But most important of all, psychological space—a feeling of security, combined with a feeling of scope for doing what you need to do and want to do, and a feeling of being plugged in to your own life, and a feeling of knowing that you matter to others. I'm certain that little children, in their own ways, need these things as much as we do.

> *a feeling of being plugged in to your own life*

J  In our zeal to help children learn things, we often crowd them in ways that are basically pretty unhealthy. I remember watching reading groups, especially with children at the lower end, watching the children wait their turns to read. Have you ever noticed their hands? Or their feet? The tenseness, the fidgeting—and then they want to go to the bathroom, or they do what adults would do if they knew their turn was coming: they look ahead and prepare their own reading instead of listening to what is being read. Some of my children like to read aloud and they beg to, but others don't like to read aloud and they don't have to, at least not in front of other children.

R The anxious behaviors you've just mentioned are so different from those you see in a secure environment where children are given space to do things that really matter to them. There the children seem so full of serious purpose, natural honesty, and joy.

J When you mention a secure environment, I think about the need that children have for an authority outside themselves, if they are to be adventurous in learning, and how important it is for that authority to seem appropriate to the children. I do set limits, and I try to communicate them as clearly as I can, but I also talk about them with the children, so that I get a sense of how appropriate they really are.

> *the need that*
> *children have for*
> *an authority*
> *outside themselves*

D If the children see the limits as appropriate, those limits become part of the social expectations that govern the classroom, rather than rules that must not be broken. Your children don't spit, not because there's a rule against it, but because they don't want to!

R There's another point about security I'd like to make. I think there's a way in which the children see you as a mother as well as a teacher. Maybe that's inevitable today, with so many mothers working outside the home, so much divorce, so much family disruption. It's easy to imagine that children are more self-reliant now, less dependent than they used to be, because they seem to grow up faster than they used to, they absorb so much information, seem so aware of things that we, as children, never were. Children can seem very sophisticated and worldly, but aren't they as young as children ever were, and just as needing of parents, especially mothers?

D Do you remember the Henry Moore sculpture we saw in that English church, Rosemary? I recall that while we were looking at it, you said that it gave you the feeling of teacher-mother, or mother-teacher.

R It's a statue of the Madonna and Child, Jeanette, but very different in character from the romantic versions that we are most familiar with. This sculpture is more than life-size, of a young mother, strong and robust. Seated on her knee is the child, of about two years, not cradled in her arms as you might expect but sitting with his back to the mother, facing the world, an expression of wisdom and innocence on his face. The child's left hand is cradled gently in the mother's, but her right hand is placed strongly and protectively on his shoulder. The mother seems to be saying, "The world is yours, but for as long as you need me I'm here—to keep you safe, to support and encourage you, to share your vision, and to let you go."

*Sculpture by Henry Moore in St. Matthew's Church, Northampton, England*

*MUSICAL INTERLUDE*

# The Book

# a Bout

# Moosk

*by Lenore and Mitsue*

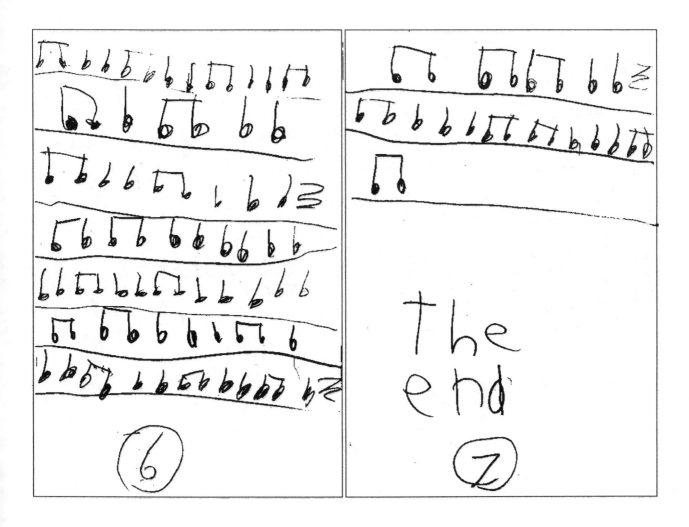

# Discussion 3

*– we talk about learning "the skills" of reading and writing –*

In our previous discussions Jeanette referred several times to the capacity of children to become deeply involved in various activities, for a few minutes, hours, days, or even weeks. She emphasized that through such involvement children learn various skills—in reading and writing, for example—more as by-products of the activity than through direct instruction. Yet I know that she does give children a fair amount of specific help with skills. I thought that it might be useful, in our final discussion, to ask her to talk about this kind of help. To get the conversation rolling I asked her how she gets children started with writing at the beginning of the year.

# *Recognizing the Reach of Their Minds*

[J] Last year, to help the children get started, I had them draw pictures, and if a child drew a boat I would ask him if he knew how to write *boat*, and of course he wouldn't, so I would ask what sounds he heard in the word, and then I'd urge him to write the sounds he heard. If all he heard was the first letter or some other letter, that's what he'd write, and if necessary I'd help him write it. This approach worked very well, but for some strange reason I didn't repeat it this year. Instead, I began by trying to *explain* this procedure to them. I started off with several examples. I said, "Maybe you're drawing a sun and you want to write the word *sun*, and so you listen to that word and maybe all you hear is the *s* and *n*, so you put that down, or maybe you know how to spell *sun*, so you put down what you know." I was trying to put them at ease with what they were going to be doing. And then I gave them two more examples— *tree* and *flower*–and I did the same thing. Well, you can guess what happened. That's all I got—*sun, tree,* and *flower*. They really learned how to spell those words! I won't make that mistake again.

[R] Just what children do when they model their writing after the pre-primers: *come, come, come, see Jack run*. Those are the words they know, and that's the style they write in.

> *the children who come to school already knowing how to read tend to write less and to write less naturally*

[J] The ones who have been pushed at home tend to write in the same stilted way. I have a child now whose paintings are beautifully creative–they're just a joy–but somehow she learned to read, probably at home, and in her writing she will not go beyond *I see the rainbow, I see the flower, I like pink flowers*. Just the words she knows how to spell. It's the least expressive writing in my room, yet I know from her paintings that there's a great deal of imagination inside her. The children who come to school already knowing how to read tend to write less, and to write less naturally, than children who come without reading. They're strongly influenced by that early knowledge of right and wrong spelling; it can be very inhibiting.

D Children need to be able to hook up some sounds with appropriate letters in order to get started. How do those letter sounds get into circulation?

J Most children come to me already knowing the alphabet, which seems to help them with their early writing. Often, when they are beginning to spell inventively, they will search the alphabet for a certain sound they hear in a word they want to write, and they will often find it in the letter name. They'll hear the \m\ sound when they say the letter *m,* and the \t\ sound when they say the letter *t,* and the \k\ sound when they say the letter *k.*

D And the \ch\ sound when they say the letter *h.* So you get *chair* spelled *hr!* Have you ever seen *church* spelled *hrh?*

J Not yet, but I wouldn't be surprised if a child did it. I do help children learn the sounds, but there isn't a certain order to it. I don't start the year saying to myself, "Now I'm going to teach this, and then this, and then that." From my experience in helping children learn to read I have an idea about the overall process and what goes into it, but I doubt that there is any particular order in which the skills should be learned. I think there is a general order, however. Most children seem to identify consonant sounds more easily than vowel sounds, and certain consonant sounds more easily than others; \s\ \z\ \m\ \t\ and \p\ for example, seem fairly easy, whereas \w\ \y\ and \h\ seem harder. With vowels most children seem to have an easier time identifying the long vowel sounds than the short ones. Right now (end of October) we've been working on long vowel sounds, and we've been working on the final silent *e* and what that does to a word, but we're also working on three-letter words with the

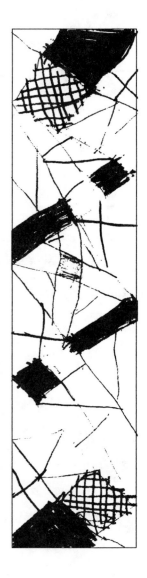

short vowels in the middle, and we're still going ahead with the consonant work for those who need it.

[D] You say that the long vowels are generally easier for children to identify than the short vowels, but the reading books usually begin with the short ones, don't they?

[J] Most of them do, but the long vowel sounds are definitely easier for most children to hear. The $\setminus \bar{a} \setminus$ as in *make* says its own name, $\setminus \bar{e} \setminus$ as in *weed* says its own name—that's probably easier than discriminating short vowel sounds: $\setminus a \setminus$ $\setminus e \setminus$ $\setminus i \setminus$ $\setminus o \setminus$ and $\setminus u \setminus$.

[R] I know you give children specific help in identifying certain sounds, but you seem to do it in very natural situations.

*we do a lot with familiar songs that we enjoy singing*

[J] We do a lot with familiar songs that we enjoy singing. I write the words on cards, and I may get a child to draw a picture of something in the song. For example, if it's "Hettie Wears a Green Dress," a child may have drawn a picture of Hettie's green dress, and we've mounted the picture on the song card, and sometime when we're singing the song I may write the word *green* on the chalkboard and ask them if they can hear the $\setminus \bar{e} \setminus$ in that word, and I point out that the two *es* say $\setminus \bar{e} \setminus$. And then if we're singing another song that has a different $\setminus \bar{e} \setminus$ word in it—maybe it's *knee*—I'll put that word on the chalkboard and point it out as another word with two $\bar{e}s$ which make the $\setminus \bar{e} \setminus$ sound, just as in *green*. So it's not like sitting down for five days and working on

*so it's not like sittting down for five days and working on $\setminus \bar{e} \setminus$*

$\setminus \bar{e} \setminus$. We might have another song, maybe with the $\setminus \bar{i} \setminus$ sound, as in *time,* and so we'll talk about that. Words like *night, bright, light* are fairly common in our songs, and so it's easy to get into the *igh* spelling of the $\setminus \bar{i} \setminus$ sound, and then *Eidelweiss* gives us the $\setminus \bar{i} \setminus$ sound spelled a different way. I point out right away that sometimes it's spelled with an *igh*, sometimes it's spelled with an *i* and a silent *e* on the end, and sometimes, as in *Eidelweiss,* it's spelled with an *ei*. I don't hesitate to bring that in, or still other spellings of \ĭ\—there are quite a few more—but I don't dwell on them. I bring them in for those children who might be ready. I find that the children are really interested in such things, even though they may not remember them the first time through.

**D** I think that pointing things out incidentally must require a great deal of restraint on your part. It would be very easy for a teacher to get carried away and turn the singing into a skills lesson.

**J** The important thing is not to labor the point, not to ruin the activity for the children. If we're reading *Charlie and the Chocolate Factory,* and we come across a big newspaper headline containing a word with a double *e* (*cheese*), I may turn the book around and show them and say, "Here's another of those words with the two *e*s," but I'm not going to interrupt the story by turning it into an exercise. What I say will be brief. Maybe I'll bring it up again at the end and maybe I won't. I try to sense the children's interest.

**R** It seems to me that this kind of contextual learning gives sounds an anchor in the children's experience. It's a very different approach from the arbitrary sequence of sounds that children often get taught.

> *contextual learning gives sounds an anchor in the children's experience*

**J** I don't think children need hours and hours of work on a sound, if we can give them one example they can remember. If they can picture that green dress and picture the word *green* because they love to sing that song about Hettie, we don't have to labor the two *e*s.

**D** When you've got the whole group around you, singing or listening to a story, and you decide to make a point about a certain word, I know you expect the children to respond orally. How do you deal with the fact that all of the children will not be ready for the point you're going to make?

nobody gets put
on the spot

[J] Well, I may say, "Here's a word with two *es* in it—can you tell me what the two *es* say?" Sometimes I call on one child, or sometimes the group, for an answer. But if it is one child, it will be a child who volunteers. As a rule I don't call on a child who doesn't volunteer. What's the point? I usually call on children who really want to do it, and very often it's a group response. There may be some children who aren't ready for it right then and others who are just beginning to get it. Nobody gets put on the spot. I very seldom get the wrong answer from children, because I don't call on children who don't know. Of course, I'm always on the alert for that child who may be hesitant to speak out, so I can give him a chance to tell what he knows. I don't just call on the children who know all the answers.

[D] Many people would say that children shouldn't be exposed to information they're not ready for. What you do seems like deliberate exposure.

[J] It is. The important thing is not that every child learns it then, but that the information gets into circulation. And in any case, who knows what a child can absorb at any particular time, things he might retrieve later and make sense of?

[R] There is a family atmosphere about all of this. I'm reminded of something I once read about violinist Yehudi Menuhin. He came from a large family surrounded by music. His parents' relatives were always dropping in, and there would be trios and quartets, and the children were growing up in this environment. It's true that they were studying music, but aside from the lessons, music was floating in and out of their consciousness, from people who knew a lot more than they did, and the children were absorbing whatever they were ready to absorb. This seems not unlike what goes on in your room.

D And in your class, because of the amount of time that the children have for their own thoughts and work, their minds have a chance to digest new ideas, in situations that are unpressured. If you labored these points and required that they be learned in sequential ways, you'd not only create pressure, you'd also virtually guarantee a certain amount of failure.

J You were asking about the specific help I give to children. One of the things I do is try to notice when a child is picking up on something that had been pointed out previously. I find myself saying, "Gee, you've really been working on the spelling of that word, and you've noticed the \ē\ sound, and you've remembered what we were saying earlier about it." Now the child may or may not have spelled the word correctly (maybe she wrote *rede* instead of *read*), and whether I point this out will depend on what I think she's ready for. In that situation the child has made a step forward. She may have put an *e* there (*rede*) instead of an *i* or an *o* or instead of no vowel at all, which she perhaps would have done several weeks earlier.

R You've mentioned ways in which you help children learn about letters and sounds. I'm wondering what the children pick up from other sources in the environment, from television programs such as *Sesame Street,* for example, or from kindergarten programs where sounds have been emphasized. I wonder also whether you notice any differences between children who come to you from a kindergarten phonics program as contrasted with children who have had a language experience approach.

J I can't say that I'm aware of an influence from *Sesame Street.* As for the kindergarten experience, I do notice that children who have had a lot of work on letter sounds seem to already know how to sound out words, but those who haven't learn quickly, if they're ready. My feeling is that children who have had a language experience approach, with some attention to sounds, tend to do a little better than those who have been drilled on individual letters, but I have no data on that.

[D] You don't ever give phonics drills, do you? Flashing a card with a *t* on it, for example, and expecting the child to say "tuh."

[J] No, I don't do that. I never teach sounds in isolation—always in the context of words the children use. As they begin to notice sounds inside of words, we may occasionally talk about what they notice. If we're talking about the \ă\ sound as in *hat*, for example, I might say, "What word do we know that has that sound in it?" and maybe they'll say *apple* or some other word. The word is something for them to hang onto in hearing the sound and remembering it. Or if it's obvious that they are hearing \b\ because they're able to generate a list of words beginning with *b*, I might then explain that *b* doesn't make a sound by itself, but you can hear it when it's in words like *bat* and *ball,* and you can feel it when your lips go together at the beginning of those words, but I don't dwell on that kind of analysis.

> *I never teach sounds in isolation*

[R] When I was teaching first grade and helping children develop these skills, I remember how powerful transformation games were.

[J] I use them a lot too. We often play the transformation game in which we generate a whole string of one-syllable words simply by changing one sound at a time: *mad mud tud tum tom toom boom broom brim.* I generally allow nonsense syllables, especially when the children are just learning. They enjoy a few minutes of this; the game swings along fast; everyone who wants to participate can do so, and no one gets put on the spot. After we've played at the chalkboard, some of the children might want to generate their own lists, and so I'll help them make up a worksheet, or they'll make up their own.

**D** A moment ago Rosemary was wondering what the children might pick up from the environment that would help them with their reading. Can you think of other examples?

**J** Recently I bought the sheet music for *The Sound of Music*—I just happened to see it at the store. I brought it in and played the songs for the children, stumbling through them as best I could (I can't sight-read very well). We sang all the songs that were in that book, and then I said, "I'll bet some of you can read some of these songs," and they said, "Oh yeah" and gathered round the piano and started following the words along. Then we got out another songbook and did the same thing with some of those songs. Then I pointed out the song cards that were posted in various parts of the room, and I said, "Maybe you can find a song you know." Pretty soon Thea said, "I think I know this song," and so she and a friend sang it, and then we started singing various songs, and many of the children were following the words along as they sang. It's interesting to me that they love reading songs, and they do follow the words.

> *they love reading songs, and they do follow the words*

**D** I suppose some people would say that when children are looking at those familiar songs or rhymes, they're just memorizing certain words, but I think there's more going on than that. The children can begin to feel their way around in the print because they know the songs, so they're in a position to soak up lots of information about sounds and spellings and about the way words look when they're written down. This kind of soaking up would probably be impossible to measure, but I'm sure it happens.

**R** Something else that would be impossible to measure is the children's growing sense of themselves as readers and their sense of power in being able to read. Even if they can't read all the words in the songs, they probably are getting images of themselves as readers, and I think that's very important in tackling a new skill.

> *this kind of soaking up [information] would probably be impossible to measure*

**D** There's a lot of complexity in these situations, and the human mind seems able to cope with it, in fact to thrive on it.

**J** It's true that children are often fascinated by complex things or things that look complex. They love silent *g*s and *k*s, for example. They catch onto them right away and can easily remember a string of silent *k* words: *knee, know, knife, knot*. And *ph* as in *telephone*—we talked about that this week and they loved it—*telephone* has meaning for them, and the idea that *ph* says \f\ is interesting; it seems to catch their imagination. And the \ī\ sound spelled *igh* as in *light, right,* and *bright* is a lot more fun than \ĭ\ in the middle of a word (*fit, sit, bit*). *Igh* is funny-looking to them, especially when I tell them that those three letters together say \ī\—and because it's funny-looking they tend to remember it. They may mix up the letters and write *ihg* or *ig,* but that doesn't matter. The point is that they're beginning to get interested in the language, and they're discovering that they can have fun with it. Why is it that children are often so intrigued by big words—*elephant, dinosaur, Tyrannosaurus rex*? Such words are interesting to them, in much the same way that big numbers are interesting—*thousands, millions, billions*. Dinosaur numbers, dinosaur words!

*dinosaur numbers, dinosaur words!*

**D** How about punctuation marks? Learning to use them correctly can seem pretty complex to some children.

**J** Apostrophes, quotation marks, and question marks. They love them, and I introduce them early, when the occasion first arises, and I'll continue to mention them once in a while as they come up. I don't labor them, and I don't expect the children to use them correctly right away. When I introduce question marks, what usually happens is that the children get so carried away that they'll use them everywhere. And when I introduce apostrophes, everything gets apostrophized.

*when I introduce apostrophes, everything gets apostrophized*

**R** Isn't that a bit like the baby who suddenly discovers what fun it is to throw things out of the pram? As many times as you put the things back, the baby throws them out. Maybe there's a play stage with question marks—when you need to put them everywhere in order to get ready to learn where to put them!

[J] Sometimes children will play at putting them in the wrong place deliberately, and they'll do playful things with spelling too. In one of her books Rhian used the word *I* many times, and each time she spelled it with a small letter instead of a capital. When I asked her why she did this, she said, "Oh, just because I thought it would be fun."

[R] Rules like that are often broken in adult life, aren't they? We often see things written without any capital letters at all, particularly in advertising and often in poetry, and it's allowable because adults are doing it.

[D] Many people would say that children must learn to do it right before they're permitted to do it wrong.

[R] But there's more involved than simply "doing it right." I think there's a necessary play stage for lots of this learning, and there's also a child's experiencing of a new sense of power, a sense of being able to do something now that he couldn't do just a short time before. I think of little Andy in my first grade class several years ago. Along about January he figured out how to spell the word *really*, and for at least a week he used the word over and over again in his writing. *I had a really good time. I really really want a new bike. I really do.* He had learned a new word that was quite hard for him to spell, and this was a way to demonstrate his achievement.

> *there's a necessary play stage for lots of learning*

[J] Really?

[R] Yes, really!

[D] Isn't there a difference between Andy's practicing his spelling of *really*, which he was spelling correctly, and

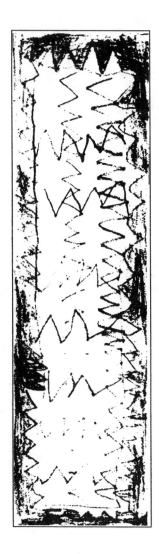

Jeanette's children practicing quotation marks, which they were often practicing incorrectly?

R   Andy was practicing *really* in a way that would not be acceptable to anyone concerned with good writing.

D   So that's bad style, but it's not bad spelling. I guess the point is that you didn't see fit to criticize Andy's style, because you knew that he was paying attention to something else which at that moment was more important to him. Still, I'm wondering about Jeanette's approach to children who play with question marks by using them more or less at random. Do you assume they will simply outgrow this, or do you do something specific to help?

J   I'll help but not while a child is playing. At that moment I might say something like, "Oh, isn't that fun!" I'll go along with the play; I won't try to make a lesson of it. I'll wait until it comes up again with the entire group or perhaps a small group.

R   Is it that the child might feel put down?

J   Yes. She might feel that that kind of play is not acceptable, and I think it should be acceptable. She's going through an important stage. But when I feel that the child is ready, I might say, "All right, take this story you've written and see if we can put in the question marks and the quotation marks." That becomes a kind of game, a challenge she's prepared to accept.

D   Can you think of other examples of complexities that catch their imaginations?

J   I think children like it when the teacher treats them as privy to information about the adult world, offbeat things that children aren't supposed to know or care about, but which they're really old enough to understand. The other day I told them about *qu,* for example. I explained that whenever we have a *q* in our language there's always a *u* after it, and that's just a rule. And then I told them that I was reading an article in the paper and that's not going to be true anymore, that there are some places in the Middle East where names are spelled with *q*s without *u*s—like the *Gulf of Aqaba* or the city of *Qom*—and that's something grownups are really going to be surprised about! Boy, they don't forget that. They know I'm letting them in on something grownup.

*they know I'm letting them in on something grownup*

|R| One way we show our respect for children is by trying to recognize the reach of their minds, their curiosity, their imagination. They know about the moon and the stars, and they're excited by that kind of information, and we don't try to protect them from it. I don't think they're confused by it; they simply make sense of it in their own ways. I get a kick out of seeing words like *Beethoven* and *Mozart* on your chalkboard.

|J| We sing several songs based on themes from Beethoven, and I occasionally play some Beethoven or Mozart to them on the record player. At some point I'll want to write Beethoven's name on the board, and I'll ask them how they think it's going to be spelled—\bay · toven\—and I'll point out that this is a word from another language, and this time the two *e*s don't say \ē\. Or Mozart. We don't say \mo · zart\. We say \mot · zart\. The children may or may not remember, but this seems to me a natural way to learn. You don't start at *a* and go straight through to *z*. Life isn't like that; it's far more complex. I certainly wouldn't expect every child in the room to know how to spell *Beethoven* or *Mozart* or even be able to pronounce them, but it's information that has a way of getting picked up and used by children who are ready for it. The point is that you can never be sure who's ready and who isn't. Recently I was showing them some of Brian Wildsmith's artwork and some of Gerald McDermott's woodcuts. The next time we did some pictures there came this one picture that was obviously very different from the others, and the child

> *it's impossible to prove in any kind of paper-and-pencil test*

said, "I tried to make it something like that one in the book you showed us." So I can see the influence of these things, but it's awfully hard to demonstrate, and it's impossible to prove in any kind of paper-and-pencil test.

R  We began this discussion by talking about what you do to help the children learn to read, and what keeps coming across to me is this integrated thing that's going on. Beethoven is making his contribution, and the woodcut artist is making his contribution. And it's all grist for the mills, and what comes out of one child's mill is different from what comes out of another's, and they use the same information in different ways, and some of them may not use it at all.

J  I'm continually being surprised by what the children pick up. I have five non-English-speaking children this year, and I have not particularly stressed the invented spelling with them yet. If one of these children draws a picture of a rabbit, I may say, "Is that rabbit jumping?" and if the child says yes, then I might write underneath the picture: *The rabbit is jumping.* More a whole-language approach to help them develop vocabulary. But it's amazing to me how much spelling these children seem to be picking up from what they see me doing with the whole group and from what they see the other children do. The other day I was working with one of the children (English-speaking) who was trying to write the word *night.* I was asking him whether he remembered how to spell the \ī\ sound, and from across the room Shin (Japanese-speaking) shouted, "*Igh,* or *i* with a silent *e* on the end." He's doing that all the time, and he's just picking it up by being attentive, and already he's on his second book and is able to spell most things without help. Last week another child (who couldn't speak a word of English in October) wrote a book about a story she had recently heard. Her title was Litte Red Writeig Hood.

[R] This experience that you're having with the non-English-speaking children is another example of how your approach differs fundamentally from the "diagnostic-prescriptive" approach.

[J] Yes. If I had diagnosed Shin in the beginning, I would have said, here's a non-English-speaking child—he is not ready for invented spelling, he doesn't have enough vocabulary, and invented spelling would only be confusing to him, so I'll just have him dictate his stories to me, and I would have excluded him from the group that was talking about the *igh* spelling. But by not excluding him I have made it possible for him to show me what he can do. The incredible thing in this kind of classroom is what the children learn from one another, things they don't get when they are working alone or in groups only with other children at their same level of English proficiency. I'm seeing some beautiful examples this year of how the English-speaking children can work with the non-English-speaking in ways that are helpful to both.

[D] I've noticed that when the children are involved in their own work—their drawing, talking, writing, painting, constructing, dramatic play, etc.—you're sometimes working with a small group that you've pulled together for some particular purpose, but much of the time you're interacting informally with the children. What do you talk about on those occasions, and what are you consciously trying to achieve?

[J] Most of our conversation is about ideas, ideas in the child's mind that are evident in his activity. I try to treat children's work—whatever it is—in much the same way that a friend of mine (an art teacher) treats children's artwork. I watched her for an entire year, and during that time I noticed how she was able to help children with color, contrast, and balance, how she did this in such nonthreatening ways, never pointing out what wasn't good, always pointing out what was. So as I go around the room

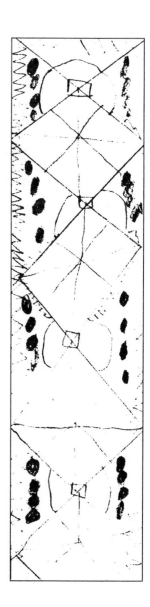

I may pick up Carla's story and say, "Oh, listen to this everybody: 'The pumpkin was moving toward the witch's door.' Does that make you want Carla to tell you what happened next?" Or I might interrupt just the children who happen to be near Carla. I'm looking for examples of ideas that seem to be going somewhere, that invite some kind of development, and I share those ideas by reading what the child has written, making it sound as exciting as I can. I don't mean that I never tell a child that something is boring—"This is a tree, this is a house, this is a flower"–I have said this, but only when a child has persisted in it. Generally I look for positive examples. But when I do this kind of highlighting, my objective is not to get that particular child to produce a more interesting story—that may happen or it may not—and at first grade I don't think I should push for it. My real objective is to get the children to begin to think about what makes a story interesting and exciting and to realize that the ideas germinating in their heads can be allowed to grow and develop and that they can be expressed in interesting ways.

> *I don't mean that I never tell a child that something is boring*

[D] To me it's significant that you talk with children primarily about their ideas, not about technical things such as handwriting, spelling, punctuation, and grammar.

[J] The more they're able to write, the more I emphasize ideas. I tend to keep the technical things separate, but I'm not rigid about it. I really try to sense what the child is paying attention to at the moment. Sometimes a child is absorbed in something technical, like how to write *b*s and *d*s, or how to use quotation marks. At another time he may be absorbed in the story he's trying to tell.

> *sometimes a child is absorbed in how to write *b*s and *d*s, another time in the story he's trying to tell*

[D] The brain gets fractured by being pulled in too many directions at once. With older children I used to emphasize the difference between what we called the "composing process" and the "editing process." We'd get our ideas down first (composing), then go back and tidy up the spelling and punctuation, and maybe the child would rewrite the paper, especially if he was pleased with what he'd written.

*J* I know many people who think that children should master the technical things first, as a kind of necessary preliminary to expressing their ideas. So the children spend their school days practicing handwriting, studying grammar in a workbook, and putting punctuation marks in somebody else's sentences. These exercises have a way of crowding out what is really important. The children may never get a chance to write sentences of their own.

*R* If they do, as in fifteen minutes of "creative writing," they tend to see this time as more skill practice rather than as an opportunity to say what's on their minds. And this is reinforced, because very often the teacher continues to comment on the handwriting or the spelling rather than the content.

*J* Everything suffers—the quality of thought and expression, the complexity of language that the children use, their interest in writing, and, of course, their output.

*D* I'm reminded of a remark made by a colleague of mine, a superb teacher of high school English. He was serving as language arts coordinator for the entire school, and we were having a schoolwide faculty meeting to evaluate the language arts curriculum. He made an eloquent little speech which contained this revealing comment: "Little children [he was referring to the primary school curriculum] should master the mechanics of writing when they're young, so that when they're old enough to have ideas worth expressing they'll be able to express them." I

> *children spend their school days putting punctuation marks in somebody else's sentences*

remember mumbling to myself that he didn't know very much about little children.

**J** Children's heads buzz with ideas, no doubt about it. The adult mistake is to think that these ideas are educationally unimportant.

**R** Adults may also think the investment in children's ideas is too risky. That's the sadness of it. They feel safer investing in the ideas of experts.

**D** I want to ask you about something Carol Chomsky said in one of her monographs on invented spelling. She said that in her opinion most children could learn to read and write pretty much on their own, if adults would be content to play a supporting rather than a teaching role, and the most supporting thing an adult can do, she said, is to answer children's questions. It occurs to me that in this discussion you haven't mentioned children's questions.

**J** I think that Carol may be referring mostly to younger children in a home situation. Younger children do ask a lot of questions, about all kinds of things, and the mother is often the only one around to answer. If I stop to think about it, well—my six-year-olds don't ask me many questions about reading and writing, but they get lots of information from each other, which probably wouldn't happen in a more formal classroom where the children aren't so free to talk and work together. Yesterday Anthony was writing in his journal (I was watching and listening from across the room), and he was asking the children everything he wanted to know: "What makes the \ j \ sound?" "How do you make a *j*?" "Which way do you turn it?" And they were answering him. I used to try to stop that. I'd say, "I want to hear Anthony sound it." Now I see that they're teaching him to read. In this kind of classroom I may be involved in sixty-seven different things, like . . . here's this child who's dying to get her book published, so I may spend

*the adult mistake is to think that children's ideas are educationally unimportant*

*they get lots of information about reading and writing from each other*

a half hour with her trying to get it ready. The others can't count on me to answer every question, so if they can get information from one another, it's probably better, and they're not seeing me as the only one who can help. They really do teach one another. Yesterday some of them were reading for Barbara and me, and some were listening to others read. I'd say, "Okay, you can read those five pages. Now can you teach them to someone else?" and the child would go over and get somebody and teach him to read those pages. I have tried to formalize this, by having a child put a marker in a book. The marker might say, "I taught Joseph to read these five pages. Signed, Tony." But formal things like that don't work. The children are interested for a day, and that's the end of it. The more informal I can keep it, the better it works.

> *the more informal I keep it the better it works*

R Like trying to keep a list of every book they've read. It soon becomes a record-keeping chore, which makes children regret they ever bothered to read the books.

D I'd like to switch to a slightly different matter, to ask you about your current views of invented spelling and its relationship to a child's development of skill in spelling.

J The first thing I'd mention is the effect on a child's attitude. There's something about the playfulness of invented spelling that leads to the enjoyment of working with words and discovering how they're spelled. This comes partly from the pleasure that adults reveal to children. It's something like when a young child learns to talk. The mother laughs with him, repeats what he says, enjoys his little mistakes, repeats them to the neighbors at a time when the child can hear. I think that does a lot for the child, and I think that when adults come into my room and read these things and smile at some of the errors and hear me say, "Wasn't that good sounding! Wasn't that good spelling!" that's encouraging to the child, not discouraging. It encourages

him to go ahead and play with words, encourages him to be interested in spelling, not afraid of it, not disliking it but seeing it as something that's fun to learn to do.

The second thing I'd mention has to do with skill. I'm sure that invented spelling does help children focus on the order of sounds in words and on the graphics to represent that order, so they are learning a skill that is basic to reading as well as to spelling. As for learning correct spelling, I'd emphasize again all the writing the children do and the fact that we're constantly editing and sending home their books, so the children are constantly seeing the correct forms, comparing their work with the edited, and doing this without suggestion from me. I often hear a child say, "Oh, so that's how you spell it!" Maybe the next time he'll spell the word correctly, or more nearly correctly.

R  One might imagine that invented spelling is some new method for teaching children to write and then to read. It's much more subtle than that. A method comes from outside the child, and, as David pointed out, invented spelling comes from inside. At one time I would have labeled this "developmental learning," and I would have meant the kind of learning that happens while a child is developing—a passing stage, or several stages. I'm seeing it differently now. I believe that we can go on learning in these deeply organic ways throughout life—if we trust ourselves and our internal capacities. If we do that, we can see within ourselves—especially when we're trying to learn something new—those patterns of natural learning that you're trying to take advantage of in your classroom, patterns that worked inside us in the early years, that enabled us to learn to walk and talk and do hundreds of other exciting things.

J  I'm glad you said that about learning. If all phonetic spelling did was turn out good spellers, I'd say drop it. For me that would not be enough to justify it. Even if that were its primary purpose, I'd question its use because we'd be wasting so much

purpose, I'd question its use because we'd be wasting so much time, because I personally don't think spelling is that important. I care much more that the children become readers and writers, that they enjoy language and enjoy using language and become skillful at using it. That's what phonetic spelling does; it contributes to these goals. But I think it also contributes to making children better spellers, and people with a healthier attitude toward spelling.

*if all phonetic spelling did was turn out good spellers, I'd say drop it*

<u>D</u> One final question, on a slightly different track. We've been talking here about your experience teaching first graders at Winn Brook School, which is in an upwardly mobile, middle-class community. Several years ago all three of us were working in schools where there was extreme poverty, and last summer you went back to inner-city Philadelphia to teach in that summer school program for poor children. Did you find that you had to teach very differently in that situation?

<u>J</u> The thing that stands out most in my mind about that summer is that the kind of education we are talking about here, the kind that seems to be working at Winn Brook, also seemed to work in inner-city Philadelphia. The children chose their activities from a fairly wide variety provided by the teachers. They made choices based on interests, abilities, stages of development. They did not choose to fool around; they chose to work and play. And in a room in which adult guidance and support were evident, they became a fairly cohesive group. They sang with exuberance, they wrote with intensity and purpose, they soaked up information about things that interested them. They enjoyed many of the same songs and stories and activities as the children back home, because, I think, they gave the cues; we watched and listened and, I believe, saw and heard. They showed us which activities were gripping to them and which were *our* ideas of what they needed. It was interesting to me that although these were city

*the same kind of education . . . seemed to work in inner-city Philadelphia*

children with limited experience of the natural world that many suburban and rural children are exposed to almost daily, some of the most gripping activities were ones centered around seashells and wildflowers. Both of these activities originated with the teachers but were a real part of the teachers' lives and shared as such (they didn't come from a curriculum guide or teacher's manual). I spent a weekend at the New Jersey shore and brought back sand and shells for a sea world display, and my intern had gone for a bicycle ride and collected wildflowers to bring in. Later we visited her home and saw the wildflowers growing. The children were sharing their experiences; we were sharing ours.

R I'm wondering if there are changes that you'd like to see in primary schools, changes that might make them more responsive to children's natural patterns of growth and learning.

J I'd like to think about that in relationship to the children I've been teaching these past three years. I think that what we've been doing in my classroom is appropriate for most of the children. But there are a few children who are not yet ready for so much focus on writing and reading, and I know that I encourage them more than I would if I didn't feel various pressures. Sometimes I'll say, "All right, we're all going to work on our writing books," and I know that these children would be better off without that expectation. I know that they would be better off talking, drawing, painting, building, working with various materials. They would come to the writing more naturally later on, and the reading too. I would like at least a three-year span for the development of the literacy skills, from age five through seven, or even eight.

R I think I hear you saying that the pressure to get every child reading in the first grade is basically destructive of the kind of education you believe in. I'm sure that many children, and teachers too, would be better off if we could free ourselves of the notion that reading is something you have to learn to do in the

> *I would like at least a three-year span for the development of literacy skills*

first grade. But this is only part of a much larger problem that's tied in with the idea of grade-level requirements and all the testing that goes along with it. If you have those requirements, then children are expected to fit them, and teachers are expected to try and make children fit. And those who don't fit tend to get rejected and labeled, which is the beginning of the failure cycle.

$\boxed{J}$ And nowadays such children are getting shunted off to specialists—to the LD (language disabilities) teachers, to the reading clinic, to the speech therapist, to the second-language teachers, to the school psychologist, even to medical doctors, who, in some cases, are prescribing pills for behavior control. A colleague of mine refers to this as "assembly-line education." Each specialist administers his or her own brand of therapy, which, on the surface, can be made to seem so sensible and wise. If we could only give children space for a more natural kind of development, they wouldn't need all that special treatment, and we'd all feel less anxious, less fragmented.

*if we could only give children space for a more natural kind of development*

$\boxed{R}$ When our director of education in Leicestershire proposed an additional year for the infant schools, his chief purpose was to extend the informal and action-oriented approach to learning. He really wanted to give children space for a more natural kind of development. Under his leadership many of the junior schools (children aged 8–11) gave up their old formality and became, in spirit and purpose, much more like good infant schools.

$\boxed{J}$ It's rare these days to hear of good early-grades practices influencing education of older children. In this country the reverse is happening. Even preschools and kindergartens are becoming first grade crammers. So often we seem to be getting children ready for something instead of letting them live fully in the present. Still, I have much to be grateful for. In my school there is at least a recognition of the problem. My principal has done his best to see that parents who don't want their child in my

kind of classroom can have a more traditional one. That of course doesn't solve the problem that I referred to in talking about the need for a three-year span, and it doesn't touch the problems Rosemary referred to when she mentioned grading and testing and the failure cycle. But even so, I'm enjoying my teaching now more than ever, and it's because of the children and the way they respond. So I'm grateful that in my school I've had support from the administration, grateful also that in my community are parents who want this kind of education for their children and are willing to work with me to make it possible.

## GEOGRAPHICAL INTERLUDE

To go to the high school, go down the hill, go straight, take a left and then go straight. 4.

*A page from Rebecca's book, school year 1996–97*

In June of 1995, a 42-year teaching career came to an end, at least officially: Jeanette Amidon retired. But not completely. In summer 1996 she said yes to two invitations from former colleagues at the Winn Brook School. She now volunteers a morning or two a week in Donna LaRoche's first grade classroom, as well as an afternoon a week in Marshall Levy's fourth grade classroom.

In these classrooms, as in Jeanette's, one finds the lively learning experiences that happen when "a group of people, adults and kids, are doing things together that really matter—to all of them." One of Donna LaRoche's particular passions is geography—she runs workshops for the National Geographic Society and seminars for local teachers. Her knowledge and interest spill over into her classroom of six- and seven-year-olds.

*Borders from*
*Yukiko's work*

The children's expressive work frequently reflects their teacher's contagious enthusiasm as well as the young child's romantic notions about places near and far. As children move through the elementary grades and beyond, they will achieve increasing levels of geographical knowledge and understanding. Although kindergartners and first graders are just beginning to acquire this knowledge, they are keenly interested in geography. And, as the work sampled here (and at the end of the color section before page 107) shows, children's geographical interests stimulate the creative expression so vital to their developing literacy.

East.

Hawe meany cuntres
will thar be from Boston
acros the oshen, to china?

Portugaland Spain, then
italy. Turkey. and travel on
the Red sea. then on the
gulf of aden, srilanka,
Past mulaya. sarawak.
tainwah, and then
Enter china in the
yellow sea.

*A page f*
*Sarah's*

# 5

## REFLECTIONS

In his book *Anatomy of an Illness as Perceived by the Patient,* the late Norman Cousins tells of visiting Albert Schweitzer at his home and hospital in Africa, and of his conversation with the doctor while there. One evening the two men were discussing African medical practice, especially witch doctors, and Mr. Cousins was marveling at their seeming effectiveness in restoring people to health.

"Some of my steadiest customers are referred to me by witch doctors," commented Schweitzer. "Don't expect me to be too critical of them." Cousins persisted, seeking an explanation for how anyone could possibly expect to become well after having been treated by a witch doctor. Schweitzer replied that he was being asked to divulge a secret that doctors have carried around inside them ever since Hippocrates. "But I'll tell you anyway," he said, his face illuminated by a half-smile. "The witch doctor succeeds for the same reason all the rest of us succeed: each patient carries his own doctor inside him. They come to us not knowing that truth. We are at our best when we give the doctor who resides within each patient a chance to go to work."

What Dr. Schweitzer said of the human capacity for health could be said, with comparable truth, of the human capacity for learning. As there is a "doctor within," so also is there a "teacher within." For parents and teachers Schweitzer's words could be felicitously transformed:

> *Each child carries his own teacher inside him.*
> *They come to us not knowing that truth.*
> *We are at our best when we give the teacher*
> *who resides within each child a chance to go to work.*

## *Back-of-the-Mind Ideas*

As mentioned in the Introduction, an important purpose of this book has been to present a classroom in which the skills of literacy are being acquired through activities and human interactions that the children find engrossing, that sustain their intellectual vitality and interest in learning, and that reflect well-established principles of child development. We have seen how young children's active minds, seeking expressive outlet through speech and the visual arts, will move quite naturally into writing as a medium of expression, and how this can be significantly stimulated when the teacher permits the children, indeed encourages them, to write and not to worry about correct spelling. It has been suggested that the mental dynamics of spelling inventively enhance children's sensitivity to speech sounds and the corresponding graphics, thereby helping them become more confident, independent readers. They may even, over time, become more confident, independent spellers.

Perhaps some of Jeanette Amidon's methods and techniques for integrating these various expressive arts will be of special interest to teachers of reading who consider themselves practitioners of what has sometimes been called the "writing road to reading," but I hope that these specialists, along with other readers of this book, will be mindful of an important message that has not, until now, been made explicit. It is that children won't write as Jeanette's children write if they are put through their paces with a prescribed writing curriculum or even if they are given a lot of ground rules and direct instruction on how to write. The same is true for their thinking, verbal expression, art, and even behavior. If Jeanette tried to teach these things in a directive way, her curriculum for doing so would almost certainly dominate the life of the classroom, depriving the children of their part in significantly shaping what happens day by day.

*Should* six-year-olds shape what happens day by day in school? Skeptics of Jeanette's "unstructured" way of working have been heard to argue that the teacher knows best, or ought to, and that a well-laid-out road map is the best way to help children reach desired educational objectives. In responding to such criticism the first and most obvious point to make is that Jeanette does structure the environment and therefore the kinds of activities that are possible in her classroom. There is plenty of structure, although of a different sort, in the way she works, and, as activities gather momentum, her input to the planning is always substantial. The second point is perhaps less obvious: Jeanette carries, in her head, a broad range of learnings, including the basic skills, that she considers appropriate for young children in their development as individuals and as members of society. Thus she sees the children moving toward a multiplicity of important objectives. But she knows from experience that this growth occurs best when children are involved in activities that engage their interest and their energy. So she carries these objectives in the back of her mind where they serve as an ongoing guide in evaluating what is happening and what the children are learning and might be ready to learn. It is this back-of-the-mind reservoir of criteria, rather than any formal lesson plan or curriculum guide, that enables her to know her children as individuals, respond to them as individuals, and evaluate their progress day by day.

## A Memorable Meeting

Evaluation of this sort is not easy to sell, or even explain, in a society hooked on test scores as the bottom-line indicator of children's educational progress. We encountered this problem repeatedly during our days with the Follow Through Project in which various approaches to early childhood education were being tried out and, presumably, tested. An independent agency had contracted with the U.S. Office of Education to do the evaluating. It turned out that our English Infant School Model gave these evaluation folks a formidable challenge, because we insisted that our educational objectives included more than teaching children to be proficient in the 3Rs, which is what the evaluation team was prepared to measure. One afternoon their man-in-charge came to visit us at our office in Boston. He wanted to find out, face to face, why we objected to standardized achievement tests for our kindergarten and first grade children. To help him understand, we wrote some of our objectives, more or less at random, on the chalkboard. The list included

- Helping children develop self-confidence and a strong sense of self

- Helping children to be self-directing

- Encouraging imagination and liveliness of mind

- Encouraging the ability to make connections and to think logically

- Encouraging self-expression in various mediums

- Encouraging the love of books and a willingness to be discriminating about books

- Helping children toward literacy in language and mathematics

- Encouraging critical thinking and a taste for problem solving

- Encouraging sensitivity to the feelings of others and the willingness to help others

- Encouraging respect for the viewpoints of others

- Encouraging the development of physical skills

- Encouraging the capacity to cope with change and the unexpected

- Encouraging respect for one's personal possessions and the possessions of others

- Encouraging honesty, forthrightness, and a sense of fair play

- Encouraging aesthetic appreciation and sensitivity to quality

- Encouraging a sense of humor

Suddenly our guest leaped to his feet, rushed to the chalkboard, and pointed to items seven and eight. "See," he said, "you folks want children to be able to read and do math. Why do you object to our testing them on those skills?"

"Because those skills are only *some* of our objectives and not really the most important," was our reply. "Some of your other program sponsors put reading and math skills at the top of their list, and that's what their teachers hammer on all day. You shouldn't be using your tests to compare us with them."

"But we don't have tests to measure these other things you folks are interested in," he said.

"That's *your* problem," we replied. "Why don't you find an experienced and insightful observer of children, hire her to go into our classrooms with a blank sheet of paper, spend enough time to find out what's going on, and write down what she observes as a basis for evaluation?"

"The answer to that is quite simple," he said. "We wouldn't be able to quantify the results objectively. We couldn't get numbers out of such an exercise, and Congress wants numbers!"

In the years since this conversation took place, evaluators have developed a greater range of observational measures. School boards and government agencies still rely heavily on standardized test scores, but alternatives exist.

## *Learning from Within*

The conversation with the man from the evaluation team lingers in memory, because it continues to signal for me so much that I believe to be wrong with schooling in America. In my view the most important things for our children to learn, in preparation for the future, are virtually impossible to measure directly, just as they are virtually impossible to teach directly. It's easier to teach children to "bark print," for example, a skill that most of them acquire in primary school, than to teach them to enjoy reading, or to value it in their private lives, or to go on reading when they leave school; it's easier to teach children to add up a column of figures and do other routine calculations than to teach them to think mathematically or to enjoy and appreciate mathematics as a way of looking at the world they live in. In general, it is relatively easy to fill children's heads with information on all manner of subjects deemed important by society, but we cannot pour into them those affections and internal coordinations of mind, body, and spirit through which information becomes transformed into useful, life-enhancing knowledge. Schools have probably always been adept at promoting "trivial-pursuit" education—the imparting of information useful on tests. Rare indeed is the school that helps children develop the full range of their powers, that moves them at the deeper levels of their being, that challenges them to become what is within them to become.

Ask most any high school student or college student to say what they're working for in school and what they're getting out of school. In one way or another, most will talk about satisfying the requirements of the system, about doing what is necessary to survive or to get ahead on the road to credentials and a career. Ask whether their studies in school have anything to do with their own personal development, with things they care deeply about, with the search for values worth living by; questions of this kind will strike most young people as quaintly irrelevant, for they do not perceive this to be what the school game is about.

The decision to do a book on Jeanette Amidon's classroom came from my belief that the traditional school game is not what our children should be playing as they prepare for the future. School, in my view, should mean experiences through which young people discover themselves and develop their own powers for getting on in an ever-changing and unpredictable world. To children, school should mean, each day, the opportunity to do things that excite their interest, appeal to their imagination, challenge their desire for competence. School should be a place where their irrepressible energy and freedom of spirit go into doing things that matter *to them*. It should not be a place where their energy gets routinely diverted into dutifully satisfying the requirements of the system, or minimally meeting those requirements, or avoiding them, or sabotaging them.

Jeanette Amidon's classroom is a place where energy is continually flowing in positive directions because children have the time, the encouragement, and the scope for doing things that matter to them and to their teacher. There is little negative energy because the teacher does not allow herself or the children to be fractured by the external demands of prescribed curriculum. It is learner-centered education that operates often in virtual defiance of the system. *What* children study makes a difference but even more important is *how* they study it: developing the skills of thought, the habits of mind and inclinations of the heart. The essence of the learner-centered approach, especially during the formative years, is what philosopher David Hawkins has called "common involvement," a partnership of adults and young people doing things together that matter to all of them—an "emerging curriculum." Because the adult brings appropriate knowledge and sensitivity to the enterprise, the things being done are worth doing, and because the young people play a key role in shaping the enterprise, the things usually get done with verve, commitment, and a genuine sense of accomplishment.

This shaping of the agenda by the child is the singular element I wish to comment on in some detail. Very young children—infants— shape their learning agendas routinely, as it is their birthright to do. They go on being self-directing, in immensely productive ways, until stalled by insensitive adult intervention. Sadly, this kind of intervention can occur as early as the first cry, but it occurs most predictably as the child reaches school age, the time when society concludes that children are mature enough to begin learning by "working" rather than by "playing." From that moment on, what the children work at is typically determined by adult authority—the teacher, the principal, the curriculum designers and textbook publishers, the testers, and even the government, all of whose authority is generally reinforced, from the child's viewpoint, by the acquiescence if not enthusiastic support of his parents. This takeover of the child's control over his or her agenda for learning brings into play, literally overnight, new rules for learning that will reshape habits of thinking and attitudes toward learning (at least school-related learning) for the next twelve years, and quite possibly for life. Let me be specific about some of these changes and why they occur.

**Inner Criteria.** Following somebody else's agenda derails the development of children's inner criteria for making sense of the world. Young children pay attention to what they are ready to pay attention to and absorb what they are ready to absorb. They are in the business of tuning their awareness and sensitivities to what feels right and to what works for their own immediate purposes. Thus, they are constantly putting newly acquired skills and knowledge to use, often to acquire more skill and more knowledge. In most schools the orientation is toward pleasing the teacher with behaviors that satisfy adult criteria about what is useful and worth knowing. Children quickly become adept at teacher-pleasing, often at the price of losing contact with their own inner sense of meaning, direction, and purpose.

**Liveliness of Mind.** Following somebody else's agenda undermines curiosity, imagination, and initiative. Most young children, greedy to understand the world, delight in asking questions and in making things happen. Their speech, often laced with unself-conscious metaphors so delightful to adults near enough to hear, reveals the nimbleness and stretch of their active imaginations. School with its typically linear curriculum and emphasis on "right answers" offers little scope for the lively and unpredictable play of children's minds.

**Respecting the Rhythms.** Following somebody else's agenda almost certainly interferes with the idiosyncratic rhythms of a child's learning: the unpredictable and unprogrammable ways in which curiosity may develop into concern, and concern into commitment; the need for active engagement or the need to withdraw; the need to seek help or the need to persevere on one's own; the need to talk with one's friends or the need to contemplate in quiet; the need to push forward with a project or the need to begin something new, or simply the need to take a rest.

**Taking Responsibility.** Always following somebody else's agenda shifts and perverts responsibility for learning. In a caring home environment, very young children, being free to learn what is appropriate at the moment, implicitly accept responsibility for their own learning, and parents (or other adults) the responsibility for helping them. The many two- and three-year-olds in my life have struck me as robust free-enterprisers, full of energy, imagination, and inventiveness, eager to test the "market" to see what it will bear, while learning from experience (if the market is wisely and sensitively responsive) about personal responsibility and about the feelings and rights of others. Such authentic responsibility for learning and self-discipline gets twisted by the command structure—the "command economy"—

of school. It makes no more sense to hold children responsible for carrying out plans they have not made, or have been conned into making, than to hold teachers responsible ("accountable") in the ways that we do for outcomes they cannot control, namely, the real learning that may or may not be going on in the minds of their students.

**A Culture of Cooperation.** Following somebody else's agenda encourages counterproductive forms of competition. The intellectual vitality of young children bubbles up from within. They don't worry a lot about who is the best walker, or talker, or asker of bright questions. Responding to the intrinsic joys of learning and doing, they are on their way to discovering, intuitively, that many things in life can be worth doing even if you can't do them particularly well. Unfortunately, the competitive environment of school tends to drive out such life-enhancing wisdom as individuals get lured into working for the gold stars—or to avoid the black marks. Such narrowly focused objectives are incompatible with the culture of cooperation so necessary for the creative growth and optimum development of the individual. In our highly competitive society most of us do not question the prevailing myth that people of all ages learn by competing.[1] While I believe it to be true that many of us do learn some things *in order to* compete, we learn very little *by* competing—except what it's like to compete!

**Avoiding Anxiety.** Following somebody else's agenda invites anxieties that impede the functioning of mind as well as body. Children are not anxious about their learning until adults make them anxious. When children are following their own pathways, in touch with their own inner criteria, they are more likely to view "mistakes" and "failures" as temporary setbacks on the way to greater success. When adults take charge, children's failures become real and anxiety-

---

[1] For a well-researched, provocative book on this subject, I suggest *No Contest: The Case Against Competition* by Alfie Kohn (Houghton Mifflin, 1986).

producing. The detrimental effects of anxiety on mental and physical functioning are almost always immediate, and frequently long-lasting, a fact now widely acknowledged in the medical and mental health professions. It is time we took it more seriously as we think about learning.

**A Sense of Travel.** Following somebody else's agenda at school, with the required grading and testing of performance, sabotages children's capacity for developing their own "sense of travel" in learning.[2] Young children, bent on learning to *do* something, like walk or swim or ride a tricycle, are typically enthusiastic about the process of learning, and buoyant when they finally succeed. They know they have traveled in their abilities, even without the gratuitous adult applause that is so frequently meant to tell them or to reward them. These same children, if constrained to learn what some adult thinks they should, become either resistant and unresponsive or dutifully compliant, looking to the adult for indications that performance is acceptable. During my years of most traditional teaching (in junior high school) the most predictable, most frequently heard question from students at examination or grading time was always, "What'd I get?" They were not attuned to their own sense of travel and not much interested in my sense of their travel; they simply (and understandably) wanted to know if they had cleared the necessary hurdles.

**Moral Values.** Finally, and perhaps most importantly, following somebody else's agenda routinely, day in and day out, as is typically the way in school, tends to distort moral development and character development. There is great wisdom in the familiar observation that one must learn to love oneself in order to love others. The high pressure, competitive hoop-jumping of school encourages socially negative attitudes and values: selfishness, pride, perhaps even arro-

---

[2] Richard Day, Hawken School's headmaster in the early '60s, often remarked to the faculty that a course is well-taught if students come through it with a firm sense of travel. We all knew that the idea is easier to proclaim than to implement.

gance among those who do well; distrust, fear, indifference among those who struggle and often fail. Children, thus preoccupied, have little chance to discover themselves as individuals and as members of a community, and thus to lay the foundation for healthy moral development, so vital to a thriving democratic society.

## *Learning & Moral Development*

The problem of how to help children acquire moral values ranks high in the minds of many people today as they think about the purposes of school in our society. Across the land voices can be heard calling for direct teaching of values and for development of supporting curriculum. Because many people subscribe to the notion that moral living and behavior must be rooted in religious belief and training, the question of teaching values in public schools tends to get politicized around the church-state issue. For me, the life of Jeanette Amidon's developmental classroom and the philosophy behind it reveal how unnecessary and irrelevant such controversies are to children's healthy growth, moral as well as emotional, social, and intellectual. The dominant ethic of that classroom is one of love and respect for the individual and of "reverence for life" (to use Albert Schweitzer's phrase) in all its forms, values widely accepted as self-evident in their validity and importance, regardless of one's religious beliefs or affiliations. It is this moral climate, rather than specific lessons in morality, that becomes truly educative in classrooms like Jeanette's.

From Jeanette herself we have already gained some perspective on how this learning occurs, but I was reminded of it again recently while talking with two individuals long associated with her classroom. One was Charna Levine, professor of early childhood education at Tufts University in Boston, who since 1976 has supervised apprentice teachers chosen to work in Jeanette's classroom The other was Vivian Zamel, director of the English as a Second Language Program at the

University of Massachusetts, who also has used the Amidon classroom as a field site for teacher training. In addition, Vivian's two children started their school careers as pupils in Jeanette's room. In the fall of 1992, while discussing life in this classroom, Charna and Vivian made some insightful observations about how values develop and get transmitted.

Vivian: Whenever I visit this classroom I'm aware that the children are having a lot of fun, and because we carry around dreary metaphors about learning having to be drudgery and tedious and work, a lot of people don't understand that because it's fun doesn't mean that there is no learning going on.

Charna: I agree with you that learning can be a lot of fun, and much of it is in this classroom, but the children do work very hard, and they struggle to master the skills in a way that may not be exactly fun, but they are motivated, in charge, and challenged. Their growth demands of them that they master it.

David: What do you mean when you say that their growth demands of them that they master it?

Charna: Well, for one thing it gives them feelings of self-esteem and confidence. The children in this classroom are appropriately challenged to struggle. I don't think I've ever seen Jeanette accept something as given. If a child is painting, she asks, "Have you finished? Which is the part you like best?" Or with a piece of writing: "Is that exactly what you want to say, or how you want to say it?" Jeanette is consistently helping children develop their own inner criteria, their own standards, and I think it's this challenge within their competence that moves them on. They trust her to know if they can do it or not. They are not scared or worried that somehow they will not measure up or that they ought to feel ashamed.

Vivian:  There are other more subtle challenges here too. There is a lot of modeling about how to be with other people. That is absent from most classrooms. Jeanette tells a child something about his behavior toward others, whether it's appropriate or not, and this happens constantly in the natural course of the life in this room, and the children really do internalize that. I've heard children here say things to each other that sound exactly like the things Jeanette would have said to them, and they say them with meaning and understanding.

Charna:  By doing this Jeanette is generating ideas about *being*. She acts as a translator of the children's perspectives of each other and their life together. Her classroom rules about *being* are generic rather than specific, so that individual children are rarely identified as transgressors. They have a chance, because of all the communication and translation, to figure things out for themselves. It gives them opportunities to save face, and it trusts them to do their best to meet Jeanette's expectations.

David:  I think that a spin-off from that, in fact an integral part of it, is that as the children become sensitive to each other's feelings and develop attitudes of fair play in their interpersonal relations, they open themselves to a quality of intellectual exchange that would not exist otherwise.

Charna:  I think that's true. Piaget said that the most important learning for children comes through dialogue at their developmental level, which is how insights often get generated, so that open communication really can be an intellectual experience.

Vivian: Having my own children in her classroom and watching Jeanette as an educator make me wish I had parenting behaviors like her teaching behaviors. What she is inculcating in the children, as Charna says, is a way of *being*. The lessons of this classroom live on with my own children. They are not lessons in a traditional sense, but I remember recently, during Martin Luther King's birthday, we were watching a program about him, and Sara remarked that Mrs. Amidon marched with Martin Luther King. The books that Sara made in this class are the ones that she goes to. She is now in the fifth grade here. Nothing that she has done in this school building means as much to her as the books she wrote here in the first grade. She has a drawer full of them, and she continues to go back and look at the books she wrote and the books that were published by the other children. These are the kinds of things that have stayed with both of my children, and they stay because the experiences meant so much to them at the time and touched them at such a deep level.

**A Letter from Melissa.** Still more recently there came to my attention yet another perspective, directly and poignantly expressed, of the underlying ethic of caring in Jeanette Amidon's classroom, an ethic that can have such long-term impact on a young person's development. The perspective comes in a letter to Jeanette, written in April 1993, from the mother of one of Jeanette's former students whose family moved to a different state after the first grade. The daughter is about to enter high school when the mother writes, as follows:

*Dear Jeanette:*

*Many times my heart has felt gratitude to you as I have delighted in Elizabeth's enjoyment of writing and reading. She is a good student, going into high school next year, who in the past has been a little shy socially—but never in her essays. I know that your careful and creative teaching is a big contribution to that. Your children always knew their writing would be appreciated.*

*Also, I remember your attitude about art, that there were no mistakes—only opportunities for something one hadn't yet imagined. Elizabeth has not found it easy to tolerate her mistakes, but she's making progress! I appreciate the good early experiences you gave her with that.*

*Mostly, I believe, it was that you loved her—as you do all of your students. You loved her with your theories of education so that she could appreciate her own ability to create, you loved her with your standards of community so that she could treat and be treated with consideration by the other students, and you loved her with your hugs so that she knew in her body and her heart that she was accepted, both when her work was good and when it wasn't. I am glad you taught my child, and wish you could teach my children's children—but the system may not let that happen!*

*Sincerely,*

*Melissa*

## Moving into Partnership

Most elementary school classrooms that I have visited in recent years have acquired the *appearance* of informality, the appearance of being learner centered rather than system centered. The children's desks are no longer bolted to the floor in straight military rows and columns. The teacher no longer spends her day "up front" orchestrating a group lesson for the entire class. Children may be permitted, perhaps even encouraged, to talk quietly with each other while working on some important project. In their happier moments many of today's teachers, especially in our "good" schools, may think of themselves as partners with children in helping them learn. Indeed, the idea of the teacher as "friendly facilitator" has been fashionable for many years, especially in early childhood circles. But there is a world of difference between motivating children to do what *you* want them to do and helping them do what *they* want to do. The former is what happens to all of us in the public marketplace where someone is forever trying to sell us something. But the marketplace is different from school. In the adult world the consumer can always refuse to buy or can buy somewhere else. In school the consumers are trapped, with little choice but to deal with those who hold power over them. Only as that power is surrendered—the power to coerce, the power to pass judgment upon, to grade, to test, to pass, to fail—only then can the mutual respect of a trusting partnership between adults and children come fully into play.

**A Classroom in New York City.** How does a teacher get into a partnership relationship with a child or group of children? It is certainly easier at the preschool level than later on when the habits and attitudes of "the system" have become deeply grooved, in the adult as well as in the child. Back in the '60s I had the opportunity to visit Sue Monell's mixed-age class of six- and seven-year-olds in the demonstration lab school of Bank Street College of Education in New York—this was a classroom very much like Jeanette's. Sue told me that she used to give her children a "choice time" in the afternoon, and it was then that they seemed most involved in what they were doing and did their most interesting work. "So I decided to shift choice time to first thing in the morning," she said. "But then there was always such a groan when choice time was up that I soon decided to let it continue, and that was how this way of working came about. I would never again go back to my old way of teaching."

**A Classroom in England.**  I experienced another memorable example of "making the switch" while in England in 1962. One of the more exciting classrooms I visited was in an upper elementary or so-called "junior school" (children eight through eleven). The school, previously very formal, was in its first year of trying to develop an activity approach based on children's interests (a classroom like Jeanette's). Teachers there referred to this approach as the "integrated day," which for several years had been the general style in the more innovative schools for younger children, aged five through seven. The particular class of ten-year-olds I visited was being taught by an experienced teacher newly freed up by the principal to try his hand in working in this new way. "I used to run a very tight ship," he told me, "but I never had the fun I'm having now." I looked around the room, rather small for 35 children, and marveled at the range of activities in progress and the hum of purposeful conversation. "However did you make the switch from formal to informal?" I asked. With a grin he replied, "If you can survive the first three months, you've got it made!"

**A Classroom in Cleveland.**  Following that visit I decided to try and work informally with a class of twenty eleven-year-olds (sixth graders) at my school in Cleveland, the Hawken School, where I had taught for many years. Hawken is an independent school with high academic standards and, at least at that time, unbelievably dedicated teachers. In the elementary grades we were in our third year of post-Sputnik innovation, beefing up the curriculum in math and science and most other subjects as well—but the faculty was far from happy with the results. In an unpublished paper written some years later, I tried to explain why.

> It is true that the children were doing more advanced work than they had done before, and they were demonstrating livelier intelligence in response to the surge of creative teaching with the more interesting and imaginative curriculums.

But they were showing this only in the classroom while the teacher was busy "motivating" them with challenging problems. If left to motivate themselves, the children didn't know what to do, their thinking stopped, and foolishness started. We also saw that the children were becoming more tense and competitive, outside the classroom as well as inside, and they were becoming less thoughtful of each other. At a faculty meeting one afternoon, Hamilton Eames, our assistant headmaster, referred insightfully to what was happening as the "rise of the new selfishness."

To most of us on the faculty it was clear that the children were being overly programmed. In our zeal to upgrade the curriculum in nearly every subject, we had encouraged the teachers to become more specialized in what they taught, which meant that the school day had to be more tightly scheduled—a time for this followed by a time for that. Sometimes it was the teacher who moved, and sometimes it was the children, but whoever moved, one activity had to stop to make way for another one to start. Not surprisingly, the concept of "pace" became the key word for quality instruction throughout the school. If a lesson was to be well-taught in 38 minutes—itself an indication of the rigors of scheduling—there had to be a beginning, a middle, and an end that produced an effective "package." As it is virtually impossible for a teacher to maintain proper pace without keeping herself at the center of the action, the children were looking to the teacher as the principal source of their intellectual stimulation and to her for the approval that made their efforts seem worthwhile. If we wanted the children to be more self-directing (which we did), to take more responsibility for their own learning (which we did), to be more compassionate in their feelings toward others (which we did), and to regard learning as directly useful in their own lives (which we most certainly did), we knew that we needed to think about ways to recapture some of that atmosphere of ease and contemplation that had so characterized the school in its pre-Sputnik days.

Inspired by my experience in England and by my desire to confront the problems just described, I received full support from Richard Day, the school's spirited headmaster, to have my sixth graders for large blocks of time each day, and to work with them in an activity-oriented program that would surely cross the usual curriculum boundaries. This meant that I was free to let the curriculum unfold, very much as Jeanette does. The experience proved to be, the most satisfying year of teaching I had experienced. The most memorable event of the year was a theatrical production presented before the entire school: a creative elaboration and spoof of a short story by Walter de la Mare, written, produced, and directed by two boys regarded by their previous teachers as "problems" and "real challenges." One of the two boys, a veteran of psychiatric counseling since preschool, had been in and out of several other schools before coming to us in the third grade. In two years with us he proved himself an exasperating yet often beguiling artist in avoiding work and conning teachers. Perhaps I was lucky, but in my room his creative brain spotted a challenge (his modernizing and dramatizing of the short story), and I was able to give him his head in developing his ideas, which became a cooperative project with the entire class. In taking charge he became a hard worker and a responsible citizen—"for the first time," his mother told me.

Interestingly, that class, including the producer-playwright, did outstanding work in *my* favorite subject, math. I guess one could say that in a partnership, everyone tends to have a healthy respect for everyone else, and passions tend to become contagious. We may not have covered as many topics and subtopics as the typical curriculum specifies that school year, but what we did was done in the spirit of inquiry and thoughtful investigation and with more wholeness of heart than I had ever before sensed in a group of children. And this was possible, at least in part, because the children were not being cattle-herded from class to class every 38 minutes.

**A Paradox.** The more relaxed approach of that school year highlighted for me an interesting paradox: that the tight programming involved in a prescribed curriculum schooling generally has the effect of demeaning and diminishing curriculum, as well as the teachers who preside over it and the children who labor through it. By contrast, a more relaxed learner-centered approach provides the time and space for committed engagement with subject matter, thereby dignifying that subject matter. It is far better, in my view, to study frisbee-throwing with a whole heart and an active mind than Shakespeare or chemistry with half a heart or no heart! It is these qualities of engagement in learning that we should be aiming for, rather than routinized exposure to or coverage of subjects specified in the curriculum.

## *Learning & Politics*

**A Government Project.** Many of us who worked on problems of education during the school reform movement of the post-Sputnik era constructed our own mental images of how schools of the future might be different and better. While we believed that what we called "the system" had to change drastically, most of us nurtured the faith that the system could be changed from within. We often talked about the need for a new vision—better yet, a demonstration—of a compelling and practical alternative to what most people, parents in particular, expect schools to be. During our experience with the Follow Through Project, Jeanette, Rosemary, and I, along with others, worked with various school districts in designated poverty areas where there was interest in learner-centered education based on demonstrated experience in certain English infant schools. As an exercise in changing the system from within, I must confess that our efforts were scarcely noticed, at least by the official evaluators.

In an evaluation of Follow Through (1981), thirteen years after the program started, Edward Zigler, the director of the Office for Child Development (which included the Head Start Bureau), reported that children in these programs did progress so long as the help was given, but they were unable to sustain their "developmental gains" when the help stopped. Said Zigler: "The clear message from Follow Through is that such programs should be extended as required during the whole developmental period of the economically disadvantaged child."[3] Although Zigler himself may not have intended to imply that the schools are basically okay and children are not, this is the most frequent assumption. Decade after decade, we go on trying to fit children to the school, not school to the children. Our message here, and throughout this book, is that enduring developmental gains are best achieved through developmental learning and teaching, not just with young children but with learners of any age. Schools, as most of us know them, are not places where this kind of learning is very often in fashion.

**A School in New Hampshire.** In 1971, after our three-year experience with Follow Through, Rosemary and I decided to pursue our vision of a better way by returning to classroom teaching, to work in a school system where bureaucratic constraints would be at a minimum. We sought and found teaching positions in a twelve-room village school in northern New Hampshire. As yet another exercise in trying to change the system from within, I would have to rate our efforts as a valuable learning experience. Edited extracts from an unpublished paper, A Tale of Two Teachers (1978), reveal significant parts of the story.

In school year 1972–73 Rosemary and I, big-city people all our lives, moved to rural New Hampshire where we both were offered teaching positions in a small (twelve room) elemen-

---

[3] *Making Schools More Effective: New Directions from Follow Through*, edited by W. Ray Rhine, with a foreword by Edward F. Zigler (Academic Press, 1981).

tary school, Rosemary in a first grade, I in a fifth. The other section of the first grade was taught by the superintendent's wife. Both the superintendent and his wife (we were told at the interview) had visited infant schools in England where they had greatly admired the informal approach to the teaching of reading, and so the superintendent was especially pleased to find Rosemary, an experienced practitioner of that approach, knocking on his door and asking for a job. He predicted that she and his wife would get on just fine (as indeed they did). As for me, the superintendent was pleased to hear of my special interest and considerable experience with innovative approaches to the teaching of English and math to older children, and he seemed not at all put off by my expressed preference for running an informal classroom. He said he thought that I would find suitable challenge in teaching one of his fifth grade sections.

On the opening day of school I discovered that I had been given 30 boys and girls constituting the more able half of the fifth grade group (as measured by the Stanford Achievement Test). My colleague in the next room had been awarded the others. To make a long and fascinating story short, I found my "bright" children so numbed by the previous four years of banal exercises and drills—in English they had done little or no creative writing, mostly copying from the blackboard; in math they were overwhelmed by the simple task of collecting and tallying their lunch money—that I decided to ignore the tightly prescribed curriculum and almost ritualistic classroom procedures to which they had become accustomed and to teach as I had planned to teach—and thought I had been hired to teach.

On reaching this decision, one of the first things I did was send a letter home to the parents, telling them that classroom life for their children was going to be a bit different from what they might be expecting, and that I hoped they would visit the classroom and talk with me about my teaching goals and ways of working with their children. To my great surprise only 4 parents out of 30 responded. What I had not realized was that parents in that school were not accustomed to visiting the school except on special occasions, such as the annual open house. Thus, I was unprepared for what was soon to happen.

Toward the end of the fourth week of school the superintendent stopped by my classroom to report that one of the parents, whom I had not met, was unhappy with my teaching of his son. Several days later, at the annual open house, this father, in rather colorful language, berated me for allowing certain misspelled words to go uncorrected in his son's creative story. Another father, comparably eloquent, lamented my failure to teach history from the textbook, beginning, as he thought proper, "with Adam and Eve." Other parents apologized to me afterwards for the behavior of these two, while at the same time expressing their strong support of my philosophy and approach.

During the next few days the town rumor mill was apparently churning fiercely as more and more horror stories about life in my allegedly libertarian classroom were being circulated. Still, no parents came to talk with me personally. The following Monday morning I arrived at school to find the friendly custodian moving desks out of my classroom. Soon, as the children began arriving, I learned that over the weekend my class had been split, the parents telephoned personally by the superintendent and given a choice: me or the retired teacher I had replaced, by reputation a strict disciplinarian who had agreed to come back at this hour of crisis. Happily, half the parents chose me.

It proved to be the most satisfying teaching year of my career—and what marvelous parent support! Of the many memorable things that happened I shall never forget the regular visits from members of the other class. During recess they would press their noses, a bit wistfully we thought, against the windows of our classroom, to watch the various activities, often including drama and dancing, going on inside. (Most of my students often chose to stay inside at recess rather than to participate in the brawls outside on the playground.) I look back on that classroom and my wife's first grade as Athenian enclaves in the midst of Sparta! We still hear from some of those parents, and several of the children, some of whom are now parents themselves.

**Three Lessons.** In retrospect the experience of that year taught three lessons. The first is that even in a small, conservative New England town there are substantial numbers of people, especially parents, who are ready to support teachers whose approach to education represents a significant alternative to traditional school. Interestingly, there are three elementary schools in this town, all basically the same, but there are several churches, all independent of each other, all free to be different. I believe that those parents who opted in 1972 for a difference in education for their children were recognizing, implicitly, that freedom of education is just as important to the health of a democracy as is freedom of religion—even though the Founding Fathers did not make this idea explicit in the Bill of Rights!

The second lesson of that year is that piecemeal efforts to change schools don't really work. No amount of tinkering with a bicycle will convert it to a motorcar! This point was driven home to me the evening of the school open house, in a conversation with the irate father who had criticized my failure to correct his son's spelling. He was the last to go home, and he wanted to talk. He wanted to know what would happen to his son the following year and whether the administration had any plans to extend my educational approach into the upper grades. He said he could go along with my philosophy if it were implemented across a span of years but not as something just "dropped in." I had to admit that I was just dropping it in. He was not reassured by my reference to Rosemary's philosophy that "a little good living is better than none"!

The third lesson of that memorable year is that a learner-centered philosophy implemented in the first grade or earlier, though threatening to some, is still far less threatening to the system than the same philosophy implemented with older children. First graders can be counted on to love a learner-centered classroom, and because the children love it their parents will be happy, which will keep the teachers happy, and the principal and the superintendent and school board. If these children are not behind in their reading compared to the "class across the hall" (which they are not likely to be), all of the adults can relax and perhaps even enjoy and be proud of this kinder and gentler way of teaching important skills. The teacher's philosophy and the broader implications of her practices can be conveniently overlooked, or never even contemplated, because those in power know that when these children enter second grade they can be quickly brought into line with the behavioral requirements of the system. It is not insignificant that Rosemary's philosophy of education and its implications for life beyond the first grade were never once mentioned or discussed by anyone in the school administration. To my knowledge such questions have never been raised or discussed at the Winn Brook School during the sixteen years that Jeanette Amidon has taught there. Even parental action in that direction has never gone beyond the wistful expression of regret that a child's life in the second grade and beyond will be so different from what it had been in the first.

By contrast, learner-centered education begun in middle school or high school is a different beast. Issues on which adults understandably disagree must be addressed and choices made. For learners of any age, a learner-centered classroom or school is very different from a classroom or school in which the learner is subordinated to a "system."

- A school staffed by teachers with passions to share (and worth sharing) and who enjoy helping children learn is very different from one in which teaching has become little more than child-minding, information-dispensing, grading, and reporting.

- A school in which children are trusted to learn through activities that matter to them is very different from one in which they are coerced or "motivated" to learn what the teachers or outside authorities say is good for them.

- A school organized to foster personal in-depth study and involvement is very different from one organized to move students en mass from lesson to lesson or class to class.

- A school that fosters the in-depth pursuit of interests is very different from one in which the interest is in passing tests and getting good grades.

- A school in which children are measured against themselves is very different from one in which children are measured against each other or against outside standards.

- A school with unlimited expectations of what learners might achieve at any age is very different from one governed by grade level requirements and standards.

- A school in which children and adults interact openly and naturally with each other is very different from one in which roles and status are sharply defined.

- A school that favors learning by doing is very different from one that favors learning by listening, watching, and reciting.

- A school in which the arts are integral to the learning process is very different from one in which the arts are peripheral or nonexistent.

- A school in which skills develop organically through activities relevant and important to the learners is very different from one in which skills are taught as isolated academic exercises.

- A school in which young people tackle problems in full and lifelike complexity is very different from one in which curriculum is fed to them in tiny sequential bites.

- A school that encourages self-discipline is very different from one in which adults do all the disciplining.

- A school in which the struggles of learning arise from identification with what is to be learned is very different from one in which the struggles are teacher-imposed.

- A school in which young people are encouraged to think critically, to wonder why, and to question established views is very different from one in which the young are protected against intellectual ferment and complexity or are indoctrinated into what is "politically correct."

- A school that is a community of learners, adults and children, doing things together that matter to them, is more likely to graduate young people who are aware of their responsibility to each other, to their families and fellow citizens, to their nation, and to the planet than is a school where the priority is to teach a prescribed curriculum, test children on it, and sort them out into winners and losers.

## *"Good Schools" Revisited*

It has been said that fish are the creatures least likely to understand the ocean, experienced astronauts the most likely to understand gravity. It is understandably difficult for most of us to imagine that school life could be very different from what we ourselves have experienced and that schools might be organized very differently from the way most of them have been organized in our lifetime. I myself had to experience a different way of working with children, as well as a different kind of school culture, before envisioning different possibilities for my own classroom. At the Hawken School near Cleveland where I taught for so many happy years, Headmaster Richard Day was fond of periodically reminding the faculty that "a good school is a benevolent dictatorship." The school was then, and I believe still is, a caring and compassionate community, but it was not truly learner-centered. In this fundamental way, it was like the public school nearby, like Winn Brook where Jeanette teaches, like most schools throughout the country. The question is, do these schools, even the best of them, provide the climate for optimal learning—intellectual, social, and moral—that will be needed in the years ahead?

I have already mentioned some unfortunate effects of a high-pressure curriculum orientation at Hawken during my experience there in the 1960s. I would like to mention two other aspects of that experience that I believe may be characteristic of life in most of our "good schools."

**Friendly Bosses.** There has emerged during my lifetime, especially in our middle-class and upper-middle-class schools, private as well as public, the merging of a culture still basically authoritarian but now with democratic overlays calculated to "motivate" children to learn what we want them to learn while making lessons interesting, relevant, even fun. This paradoxical mix casts teachers into the ambiguous role of being friend as well as boss. In my experience what tends to result is an uneasy balance and contest of wills between children and teachers, a contest characteristically friendly, hostile only when things really go wrong. Bill Hull often remarked that "Teaching a class of fifth graders at the Shady Hill School in Cambridge was like trying to ride a greased ball." Ditto for me at Hawken (until the year of my learner-centered experiment). This is not to say that a greased-ball classroom doesn't work; it does, but not efficiently, because there is simply so much human energy (not to mention money) being shunted into counterproductive, or minimally productive, activity. Nor is it to say that a greased-ball classroom isn't educational; it is, but it is education for a society of upwardly mobile competitors, negotiators, and manipulators, not education for a society of individuals with a social conscience and a commitment to a lifetime of learning.

**Disadvantaged Academics.**   Many people who are critical of schooling in America seem to believe that the casualties of the system—the "disadvantaged," the handicapped, the failures, and the dropouts—are the ones for society to worry about, whereas those who do well in school are getting "quality education." After spending the first fifteen years of my teaching career in a school densely populated by "winners," I see the problem in somewhat broader terms. Winners in school are usually those who are skillful with words and numbers—language and mathematics—the skills most critical to getting into college and of doing well while there. What I noticed in my teaching, year after year, was that my "best" students, those who got the highest grades, were often not the most creative thinkers or problem solvers. The high achievers were skillful producers in response to schoolish assignments and routine problem solving, but they were often short on curiosity, creativity, and inventiveness. My colleague, Hamilton Eames, ever nimble with words himself, shared this perception and was fond of remarking that children with a gift for words and numbers are afflicted with the "fatal facility": fatal because the ease of getting good grades has a way of short-circuiting the intellect and of disengaging the heart. While at the Shady Hill School, Bill Hull studied children's thinking in a variety of classroom situations over a number of years. In one of his unpublished reports he tells of working in a classroom of third graders one year, then two years later teaching the same children as fifth graders. He noticed, regrettably, that many of those same children, so lively minded as eight-year-olds, had given up thinking and become "production artists" by age ten. When the payoff is for production, as in school it generally is, there is little incentive to keep the creative brain alive. For those of us skillful in playing the school game (a game that continues into college), it is difficult to avoid becoming a disadvantaged academic.

It is frequently noted that the Einsteins and Churchills of this world did poorly in school. (No doubt they resisted becoming disadvantaged academics!) The paucity of such types is no reason not to take seriously the lesson of their experience. If America is to flourish in the years ahead, our schools must do far more than reduce the dropout rate and the incidence of illiteracy in English, math, and science. We must address the problem of wasted human potential throughout the school population, in our prosperous schools as well as in those victimized by poverty. There is no doubt that the "savage inequalities" in American schooling so vividly described by Jonathan Kozol[4] serve to dramatize our most urgent needs and to clarify what our priorities ought to be. While these schools of degradation and neglect desperately need what only money can buy, to repair the plumbing and mend the leaking roofs, they also need much that money cannot buy, a caring and respect for the individual child and a school life that promotes growth rather than failure. It is my belief that what our "good schools" need to make them better is, in

---

[4] Kozol, Jonathan, *Savage Inequalities* (Harper Perennial, 1991).

principle, what our forgotten children need to help them survive. They need an educational life that is rooted in the principles of development. They need freedom to be engaged in what facilitates their survival and their growth. Unfortunately, what most children get, except in classrooms like Jeanette's, is an imposed curriculum and a system of grading, testing, and sorting out that is designed to generate failure.

**Freedom to Learn.** As we think about what happens to children in school, what is really at issue is whether young people *should* be free to learn and what freedom to learn *really means.* In thinking about that it may be helpful to ask whether children should be free to play sports. Most of us would probably say that they should, which is why school sports are so popular and why we have such good teams. When I first began teaching at Hawken back in 1949, every boy (it was then a school for boys) from grades four through nine was required to participate in sports during what was called the afternoon "play period." It was a requirement that produced as much counterproductive activity as any untimely effort to drag children through a lesson in math, or science, or art. It wasn't until we made sports elective and offered other outdoor options, and occasionally some indoor options, that we began to get quality participation in sports and in the other activities as well.

The basic psychological reality is that freedom to learn sports is not that different from freedom to learn math, or science, or art. Freedom to learn is not freedom *from* discipline but freedom *to accept* the discipline of the enterprise at hand. It is not freedom *from* responsibility but freedom *to be* responsible. When we require children to be responsible for learning what we think they should learn, we invite them to be irresponsible. The key question is, under what conditions will young people put optimum energy into learning and accept the responsibility and discipline involved? Again, the answer is not all that difficult: get rid of all the dead or half-dead ideas that clutter their line of travel. Get rid of the idea that exposure to a subject means learning, or that learning necessarily comes with "covering the textbook," with doing lots of homework in the subject, or even with passing a test on the subject or getting a good grade. Get rid of the idea that staying in school, or getting a diploma, or scoring high on standardized tests means learning. If we could get rid of such cosmetic froth, or at least recognize that it is cosmetic, we could free up ourselves, and more of our young people, to begin paying attention to the inner realities of learning.

Most children don't need to be "motivated" to learn. They are learning, and they want to go on doing it. With modern communication they know now, as perhaps never before, that there is an exciting world out there to learn about; they want their share of the excitement; they hate being bored. At the same time there is, for all young people, the demanding world up close to understand and to manage, the world of their own personal development, with its continuing newness, mystery, and challenge during the first two decades of life. In coping with this inner world they want to feel in charge—but they do not want to feel alone in their in-chargeness. An education genuinely learner-centered reflects the individual's response to both worlds and manifests their inevitable blending—always, I would emphasize, within the social context—and it reflects the ongoing development of the individual as her kaleidoscopic needs and energies unfold.

This need to become a confident, self-directing individual is, at some level of awareness, the irresistible compulsion of every normal young person. It is for all of us, especially during our formative years, our nature-given "curriculum." Today, as children's lives outside of school are becoming more and more fractured and destabilized, an imposed curriculum, and the factory organization required to dispense it, have become increasingly irrelevant to the real concerns of our young people. There is unprecedented need and opportunity for schools to become what few have ever been: havens of meaning, relevance, and genuine caring, which I conceive to be the foundation of real intellectual, social, and moral development. If schools could become that, we would not only have less crime in the streets but we would also have better scientists and mathematicians, better craftsmen and tradesmen, better poets and philosophers, better mothers and fathers.

## *A Plan for Continuing Growth*

I imagine that in learner-centered schools of the future this kind of curriculum will be, as in Jeanette Amidon's classroom, an unfolding of individual and group travel through activities, projects, and topics of study that reflect individual needs, that challenge in appropriate ways the individual's desire for competence and achievement, that galvanize the individual into constructive action, hard work, and commitment. Such learner-centered education will produce energy flows in positive developmental directions, and it will be by such energy flows—children's excitement and involvement in learning—that these schools and teachers will be properly judged.

Evaluation, as always, will be critically important, and in these schools and classrooms it will be the ongoing evaluation integral to the teaching/learning process that will be most important, because this kind of evaluation will be carried out by the children themselves, in cooperation with their teachers and parents. Standardized testing, for those that want it or feel they need it, could be available as an extracurricular activity.

Such learner-centered education implies, as through this book we have tried to demonstrate, a transformation of the traditional client-patient relationship so familiar to all of us in the doctor's office as well as in the classroom, a transformation through which learning becomes an enterprise of partnership, of teachers and young people working together in an atmosphere of freedom, mutual caring, and respect. To achieve this quality of partnership, schools must have autonomy, so that teachers can have autonomy, so that young people can have autonomy. In the "classroom of the mind"—the scene of the action that really matters—everyone needs to feel needed *and* to feel in charge.

How to extend developmentally appropriate practices in education to classrooms and schools where they do not at present exist is among the thorniest of questions. I believe that developmental education is much like effective democracy: it cannot be spread either by force or by precept. It is a way of thinking and believing and acting, and it can only grow organically. But it can be helped to grow, most significantly by encouraging it where it exists, as in classrooms like Jeanette's and in alternative schools like those pioneered by Deborah Meier in New York's District Four. These are but a few of the many growth points across the land that need to be nourished and, where possible, replicated, in a practical long-range plan for continuing growth.

## *In a Few Words*

As I think about the problem of school change and the need for significant choice between contrasting approaches to education, I find it useful to contemplate a formulation of learner-centered objectives that might free up our good schools to become even better and our poor schools to escape the shackles of the traditional teach-and-test curriculum. I look for words that will lure us *beyond words* in the re-creation of school life that challenges and respects the full range of a young person's powers, that fosters the development of skills, attitudes, and values needed for a lifetime of learning, that puts human feeling and morality at the center of the enterprise. I look for a formulation brief, trenchant, comprehensive. What words can possibly meet this challenge?

One of the more celebrated teachers of all time, the Greek philosopher Socrates, said it in just two. For him the essence of education and the height of wisdom was to *know thyself,* which he believed would encompass a life of personal and civic virtue amongst the citizens of ancient Athens. Five hundred years later another great teacher was said to have experienced an internally focused education, described in the New Testament as follows: "And Jesus increased in wisdom and stature, and in favor with God and man"— balancing growth of mind, body, heart, and soul. In our own century another great teacher, the eminent British philosopher, Alfred North Whitehead, emphasized the internal side of growth and achievement when in 1929, in *The Aims of Education,* he wrote:

> *Culture is activity of thought,*
>
> *and receptiveness to beauty*
>
> *and humane feeling.*

How better, in so few words, to express the coming together of intellect, feeling, and morality that moves us when we are living fully, growing, and learning? How better to describe, briefly, the culture of a classroom and an entire school, in which all individuals are equally valued, appropriately challenged, and helped to develop in their own unique ways?

# EPILOGUE

*When we try to pick out anything by itself,*
*we find it hitched to everything else in the universe.*

— John Muir

As we have been exploring the ever-widening implications of a "living classroom," I am reminded of two recent books that I find extremely provocative. One deals with the evolution of the human species, the other with the evolution of human culture, what we sometimes loosely refer to as "civilization." In the first book, *The Evolution of Consciousness*, author Robert Ornstein points out that the human brain, in size and complexity, has probably changed very little since our ancestors first decided to walk on two legs instead of four. He also suggests that the higher powers of the human mind, our powers of reasoning, contributed little to early man's capacity for survival, which put a premium on acting swiftly (to avoid being eaten) rather than on taking time to think things through. He goes on to suggest that this is precisely the way we humans have continued until today to use our much-vaunted powers of intellect. Most of us mobilize our brain power to enhance our immediate well-being and to deal with what we perceive as short-term threats to personal security and survival. Examples are not difficult to think of:

"tomorrow's job thinking" by our employed and unemployed,

"next dividend thinking" by our savers and investors,

"quarterly report thinking" by our business leaders,

"tomorrow's headline thinking" by our journalists,

"next election thinking" by our public officials,

"next channel thinking" by the viewers, and of course

"tonight's homework, tomorrow's test thinking" by our children in school.

Ornstein argues that this short-term orientation won't work, or should not be seen to work, any longer, because now, for the first time in the history of all species, one species (our own) has developed the capacity to transform the environment it depends upon for survival. If we continue to exploit and degrade our planet, to overpopulate it, and to ever-diminish its finite resources, we shall eventually destroy ourselves and our home. He calls for an evolution of consciousness, a reorientation of our powers of learning and awareness toward the requirements for surviving and prospering in the long term.

The cosmic sweep of Ornstein's message nonetheless has rather direct bearing on our discussion here. First, of course, is his emphasis on the education of consciousness: I see classrooms like the one described in this book as tiny cells representing the incipient growth toward a new consciousness, a classroom in which the adults are devoted to helping children discover themselves as individuals and as responsible members of a functioning community. Second is his emphasis on the problems of cultural and species survival, which surely must become our priority agenda for the future. If the school-based education of young people were to become quite properly learner centered, could we then not trust these same young people to continue to develop their inner powers, using them in responsibly confronting the problems that beset us as a society and as a species? In conviction derived from some degree of relevant experience, my answer to that question is an emphatic YES.

In the other thought-provoking book, *The Chalice and the Blade*, author Riane Eisler, a lawyer turned anthropologist, reports on her search of the literature on anthropology, which of course deals with how human beings have lived during the relatively recent past, say the last ten to twenty thousand years, a minuscule fraction of the time since our brain grew to its present enormous size. From her studies Eisler concludes that the established anthropological view about what life was like in primitive, preagrarian societies is quite wrong:

that they were not societies in which men dominated over women, or women over men. They were not dominator societies at all, but *partnership* societies. Domination, generally male, came in with the agrarian revolution. I don't recall that children get much mention in this book, how their dominated status has probably a longer history than that of women, but I doubt that the inclusion of children would alter Eisler's view that a return to the "partnership model" must be the wave of the future, if our civilization, and perhaps even our species, are to survive. Perhaps she would be cheered by the example presented in this book, of a classroom of young children in which the spirit of partnership, of each with all, is so pervasive in all that happens.

As a teacher, parent, and now grandparent, I am reassured by the thought that evolution, human and cultural, is on my side. My hope is that now, as our society struggles in disappointment over what our schools seem not to be accomplishing, we will be encouraged by that growing number of enclaves where education is being approached differently and where the dynamics of child development, indeed of human development, are being taken seriously. My belief is that this growing number of "living classrooms," in which parents and teachers are ever mindful of the *teacher within,* are already showing us the way to the future.

# BACKGROUND READINGS

*– some personal favorites, annotated –*

Borysenko, Joan. *Minding the Body, Mending the Mind.* Addison-Wesley, 1987.

> The author, director of the Mind/Body Clinic of the Harvard Medical School, describes in readable, practical ways how an individual's mental and physical states interact in generating conditions of sickness and of health. The connections to a healthy environment for learning are not difficult to imagine.

Coles, Robert. *The Political Life of Children.* Houghton Mifflin, 1986. *The Moral Life of Children,* 1986. *The Spiritual Life of Children,* 1990.

> On page 47 of *The Living Classroom* I remark that "the children's work is a constant reminder that their heads are humming with serious concerns." Readers seeking additional evidence of children's mental life will find it in rich and graphic abundance in this long-term study based on Coles's in-depth conversations with children in various cultures. The three-volume series is subtitled *The Inner Lives of Children.*

Dennison, George. *The Lives of Children.* Random House, 1969.

> At the First Street School in New York's Lower East Side teacher/researcher George Dennison describes how children born into poverty, neglect, and abuse can be saved, at least temporarily, by adults who respond to them as individuals rather than as objects of instruction. "If, as parents, we were to take as our concern not the instruction of our children but the lives of our children, we would find that our schools could be used in a powerfully regenerative way" (p. 6). A powerful and insightful book, as urgently relevant today as when first published.

Dewey, John. *The Child and Curriculum* and *The School and Society.* University of Chicago Press, 1902.

> On rereading, after many years, America's most celebrated educational philosopher, I find these two classic essays lucid, pungent, and astonishingly relevant to today's educational issues. Based on talks to parents at the University of Chicago Elementary School, these short essays, nearly a century old, bring useful historical perspective to educational issues of Dewey's day and our own.

Edelman. Marian Wright. *The Measure of Our Success: A Letter to My Children.* Beacon Press, 1992.

Making scant reference to schools and schooling, Ms. Edelman, the founder and president of the Children's Defense Fund, writes of moral and spiritual values needed by our children and by all of us if our society, and indeed our civilization, is to thrive in the next century.

Elkind, David. *The Hurried Child.* Rev. ed. Addison-Wesley, 1988.

In this readable, nontechnical work, psychologist David Elkind lucidly describes the currents of contemporary American culture that make children the victims of adult pressures and anxieties. He explains the natural stages of children's growth and learning that are thus violated, to the long-term detriment, he believes, of our strength as a nation. Incidentally, Professor Elkind visited Jeanette Amidon's classroom and subsequently used videotape footage from that visit in one of his teacher training films.

Erikson, Joan M. *Wisdom and the Senses.* W.W. Norton, 1988.

This profoundly human and humane book, beautifully written, puts artistic creativity and the integrity of the senses at the heart of personal growth and the educational process, from infancy onward. Weaving insights of her own into the fabric of her husband Erik Erikson's theory of the life cycle, the author projects a vision of human potential within which learning is perceived as a lifelong adventure.

Faber, Adele, and Elaine Mazlish. *Liberated Parents, Liberated Children.* Avon Books, 1974. *How to Talk So Kids Will Listen and Listen So Kids Will Talk*, 1980.

These companion volumes, wise and practical on every page, implicitly speak to the difference between treating children as people and treating them as objects. The implications for human relations in the wider domain, and for education at all levels, cannot easily be ignored.

Featherstone, Helen. *A Difference in the Family.* Basic Books, 1980.

Jody was the most severely disabled child I have ever known up close. In this remarkable, erudite book his mother reveals, with courage and frankness, how through nine years of loving care the pain and anguish of her son's disability reshaped the lives of the entire family. An important book about learning and growth.

Featherstone, Joseph. *Schools Where Children Learn.* Liveright, 1971.

The deepening malaise of our schools during the quarter century since this book was published only serves to enhance the historical perspective brought by the author to this lucid account of exemplary educational practice in a small number of schools representing significant alternatives to the traditional mode.

Feynman, Richard P. *Surely You're Joking, Mr. Feynman: Adventures of a Curious Character.* W.W. Norton, 1985. *What Do You Care What Other People Think? Further Adventures of a Curious Character,* 1988.

I include these two delectable books (autobiographical) by one of this century's most memorable and creative scientists as an indication that traditional schooling has little or nothing to do with the education of genius.

Fliegel, Seymour, and James MacGuire. *Miracle in East Harlem: The Fight for Choice in Public Education.* Random House, 1993.

This is the story of an adventure in public school choice involving, at recent count, more than two dozen small alternative schools in one of New York City's poorest neighborhoods. An honest, insightful, warmly human account of the "politics" of putting children first, and of the rich rewards that follow. If it can be done in New York City . . . .

Freire, Paulo. *The Politics of Education.* Bergin & Garvey, 1985.

"There is no other road to humanization . . . other than authentic transformation of the dehumanizing structure [of education] . . . . The adult literacy process demands among teachers and students a relationship of authentic dialogue . . . . Even if [illiterates] can occasionally read and write because they were 'taught' in humanitarian—but not humanist—literacy campaigns, they are nevertheless alienated from the power responsible for their silence" (pp. 49–50).

Although Freire, world-renowned teacher and educational pioneer, is speaking here about literacy campaigns in the Third World, his ideas have provocative relevance to literacy education and to human development everywhere.

Gallwey, W. Timothy. *The Inner Game of Tennis.* Random House, 1974.

"There is a far more natural and effective process for learning and doing almost anything than most of us realize. It is similar to the process we all used, but soon forgot, as we learned to walk and talk . . . . This process doesn't have to be learned; we already know it. All that is needed is to unlearn those habits which interfere with it and then to just 'let it happen'" (p. 13).

Gatto, John Taylor. *Dumbing Us Down*. New Society, 1992.

> In this fiercely forthright description of the damaging "hidden curriculum" inherent in the way most schools operate, this celebrated veteran teacher (voted New York State's Teacher of the Year) helps us understand how schooling, as most of us know it, is antithetical to education. The reforms proposed are truly revolutionary.

Gelb, Michael. *Body Learning*. Delilah, 1981.

> In this eminently practical book, based on the ideas and techniques of F.M. Alexander, the author describes how growth-restrictive habits of mind and body get established and how, through the art of not-trying, they can be overcome. Although the focus is on the learning of physical skills, one cannot fail to notice the wider implications.

Gordon, Julia Weber. *My Country School Diary*. Dell, 1946. (I recommend the 1970 edition, which contains an introduction by John Holt.)

> This book reveals a master teacher at work, free to be guided solely by her sense of her children's total developmental needs. A beautifully sensitive, insightful, and practical work. "In the months that have passed many things have happened. I have watched the personalities of these children begin to emerge and become somewhat free. I have watched them grow in ability to plan, to carry out their plans successfully, to recognize and to solve their problems. I have watched them grow in their ability to live together and to respect each other. I have encouraged many kinds of activities so that each child would be challenged by one at least and so find his place in our group" (p. 48).

Hawkins, David. *The Informed Vision*. Agathon, 1974.

> As philosopher, scientist, teacher, and lifelong student of the learning process the author writes eloquently, but always with the common touch, as he explores the educational implications of human development.

Hawkins, Frances Pockman. *The Logic of Action*. Pantheon, 1969.

> In this delightful book by a wise and resourceful teacher we gain fresh insight into the nonverbal roots of intellectual and social development in a class where children learn by doing, assisted by a teacher who is a master of responding to them as individuals. These young children at work are six preschoolers who are deaf.

Hayek, Frederick A. *The Road to Serfdom.* University of Chicago Press, 1944.

As traditional schooling represents, in my view, the imposition of "centralized planning" on the lives of "consumers" (children), readers of *The Living Classroom* may wish to contemplate the relevance to education of Professor Hayek's classic work in defense of individualism and free enterprise.

Hoff, Benjamin. *The Te of Piglet.* Penguin, 1992.

If you have never thought of Eeyores as educators, read pages 70–75, and then go on, as I did, to read the entire book. If you do this, I guarantee you'll buy its predecessor, *The Tao of Pooh.*

Holt, John. *How Children Fail.* Pitman, 1964. *How Children Learn,* 1967.

A valued friend and colleague, the late John Holt, wrote many fine books on education, of which these two remain my favorites. An astute observer of children with a gift for saying important things simply and clearly, Holt invites us to treat children as people (as we all like to be treated) and to savor the life-enhancing consequences.

Kelley, Earl C. *Education and the Nature of Man.* Harper, 1952. *Education for What is Real.* Harper & Row, 1947.

In their clear and cogent lines of argument these little classics remain as timely and vital today as when first published a half century ago.

Kohl, Herbert. *36 Children.* New York: New American Library, 1968.

In this and in more recent books, this great teacher brings us close to children demonstrating alternatives to much that is irrelevant to children in traditional schooling. A gem of a book, not to be missed (written with Judith Kohl) is *The View from the Oak,* the story of a little "school" in Herb's backyard.

Kozol, Jonathan. *Savage Inequalities.* Harper Perennial, 1991.

The voices of America's rejected and forgotten children, their parents, and their teachers speak through these pages of penetrating and passionate reporting as Kozol documents, yet again, how equality of opportunity is

Maslow, Abraham H. *Toward a Psychology of Being.* 2nd ed. D. Van Nostrand, 1962.

While describing the inherent limitations of both behavioristic and Freudian psychologies, Maslow pioneers a "third way" psychology based on the powers and "self-actualizing" capacities with which human beings are, by nature, endowed.

McCluggage, Denise. *The Centered Skier.* Warner, 1977.

From a book that is not just about skiing the thoughtful reader gains insights into how the wisdom of the East can contribute to the culture of the West in ways that enhance human learning and optimize performance.

Paley, Vivian Gussin. *White Teacher.* Harvard University Press, 1979.

In this book, her first, as in her other more recent titles, Vivian Paley explores her own learning about how children learn, in ways that are charming, illuminating, and inspiring. Her work reveals the unique qualities of classroom-based "personal research" as conducted by a dedicated and gifted teacher.

Richardson, Elwyn S. *In the Early World.* Pantheon, 1964.

Perhaps there has never been a better book than this one for those interested in the dynamics of children's expressive growth and its integration with their intellectual, social, and moral development. The climate of "cooperative individualism" characterizing the author's classroom and school inspires a vision of what schools could become, and need to become, in a democratic society.

Rogers, Carl. *Freedom to Learn.* Merrill, 1969.

This pioneer of client-centered therapy speaks simply and eloquently, from a lifetime of experience, about the organic/biological roots of human learning and about human values as a function of personal autonomy and freedom.